the devil,

the lovers,

& me

the devil,
the lovers,
& me

my life in tarot

kimberlee auerbach

DUTTON

PUBLISHER'S NOTE: Some names and identifying details have been changed, some characters are composites, and time has been compressed for dramatic effect.

DUTTON
Published by Penguin Group (USA) Inc.
375 Hudson Street, New York, New York 10014, U.S.A.
Penguin Group (Canada), 90 Eglinton Avenue East, Suite 700, Toronto, Ontario M4P 2Y3, Canada (a division of Pearson Penguin Canada Inc.); Penguin Books Ltd, 80 Strand, London WC2R 0RL, England; Penguin Ireland, 25 St Stephen's Green, Dublin 2, Ireland (a division of Penguin Books Ltd); Penguin Group (Australia), 250 Camberwell Road, Camberwell, Victoria 3124, Australia (a division of Pearson Australia Group Pty Ltd); Penguin Books India Pvt Ltd, 11 Community Centre, Panchsheel Park, New Delhi – 110 017, India; Penguin Group (NZ), 67 Apollo Drive, Rosedale, North Shore 0745, Auckland, New Zealand (a division of Pearson New Zealand Ltd.); Penguin Books (South Africa) (Pty) Ltd, 24 Sturdee Avenue, Rosebank, Johannesburg 2196, South Africa

Penguin Books Ltd, Registered Offices: 80 Strand, London WC2R 0RL, England

Published by Dutton, a member of Penguin Group (USA) Inc.
First printing, August 2007
10   9   8   7   6   5   4   3   2   1

 REGISTERED TRADEMARK—MARCA REGISTRADA

LIBRARY OF CONGRESS CATALOGING-IN-PUBLICATION DATA
Auerbach, Kimberlee.
The Devil, the lovers, & me : my life in tarot / Kimberlee Auerbach.
    p. cm.
ISBN 978-0-525-95021-9 (hardcover)
1 Tarot.   2. Auerbach, Kimberlee.   I. Title.
BF1879.T2A935 2007
133.3'2424—dc22   2007016087

Illustrations from the Rider-Waite Tarot Deck® reproduced by permission of U.S. Games Systems, Inc., Stamford, CT 06902 USA. Copyright © 1971 by U.S. Games Systems, Inc. Further reproduction prohibited. The Rider-Waite Tarot Deck® is a registered trademark of U.S. Games Systems, Inc.

Grateful acknowledgment is made to the following for permission to reprint:

"All I want," words and music by Joni Mitchell © 1971 (renewed) Crazy Crow Music. All rights administered by Sony/ATV Music Publishing, 8 Music Square West, Nashville, TN 37203. All rights reserved. Used by permission of Alfred Publishing Co., Inc.

"The Circle Game," words and music by Joni Mitchell © 1966 (renewed) Crazy Crow Music. All rights administered by Sony/ATV Music Publishing, 8 Music Square West, Nashville, TN 37203. All rights reserved. Used by permission of Alfred Publishing Co., Inc.

The line from "i love you much (most beautiful darling)." Copyright © 1958, 1986, 1991 by the Trustees for the E. E. Cummings Trust, from Complete Poems: 1904–1962 by E. E. Cummings, edited by George J. Firmage. Used by permission of Liveright Publishing Corporation.

Printed in the United States of America • Set in Bembo • Designed by Spring Hoteling

To my mother, who was told to never tell. May this set us free.

TEMPERANCE.

THE HIGH PRIESTESS.

JUSTICE.

THE FOOL.

DEATH.

WHEEL of FORTUNE.

THE LOVERS.

THE DEVIL.

THE SUN.

THE WORLD.

THE EMPRESS.

THE TOWER.

contents

prologue

Cement lions. I'm a Leo. It's a sign! I pet
each one on the head as I run up the steps of Iris's brown-
stone building on West End Avenue between Ninety-first
and Ninety-second streets. It's a thick August night, 10 P.M.,
not that late, but the street is empty and eerily quiet. As I
reach the top of the stoop, I see the shadow of a man round
the corner. My stomach tightens. It's not as if I'm new to
the city. I'm thirty-three and have been living here for
eight years. I'm a big girl. Five-eight. Size 10 shoe. Not
easy prey. But my apple cheeks and Bambi eyes make me
look less like a streetwise New Yorker and more like a farm
girl from Nebraska.

I glance at Iris's business card. Apartment #9. *Nine is
my favorite number!* I push the button, and she buzzes me in

a second later without asking my name. *Of course. She's clairvoyant. Or the intercom is broken. What if the intercom is broken? What if she lets anybody in? What if the man on the street comes in after me? Calm down. There are lions. There's the #9. It's fine.* I make sure the door is closed behind me and climb the steep, carpeted staircase.

When I get to the third-floor landing, I spot Iris's black lacquered door. I knock once and wait. I knock again. No footsteps, no shuffling, nothing. Then without warning, the door swings open, and Iris stands there, still as a morning lake, as though she's been there the whole time.

She is a small woman, but her presence could fill a stadium. I don't know why, but I thought she would be big and fat and wearing an oversized purple dress, adorned with blown-glass jewelry, like some new-age earth mother spirit goddess. Instead, she is wearing red lipstick, wire-rimmed glasses, a white cotton button-down and crisp, black capris, making her look more like a European ballet teacher—chin up, shoulders back, silver hair tied tight in a bun. She strikes me as someone who would eat a mango with her bare hands, yet spend hours lovingly ironing her linens.

"Are you going to stand there all night?" she asks in a surprisingly deep voice.

"Sorry. Hi. I'm Kimberlee," I say, and reach out my hand to shake hers.

"I know who you are. We have an appointment."
Right.

Iris waves me in, then glides across the marble floor

into her living room where there are candles on every surface.

"How long have you been here?" I ask.

"A long, long, long time." By the tone of her voice, I'm not sure if she's talking about the apartment or her many lives on Earth. "Please take a seat. I'll be right back," she says, and leaves the room.

I place my purse on the floor and sink into the navy velvet armchair, feeling my belly jut out over my I-can't-really-get-away-with-such-low-cut jeans.

Everywhere I look, there's a relic from another country, another time: a threadbare turquoise kimono in a shadow box; a unicorn tapestry hanging above the fireplace; black-on-black pottery, the kind I saw when I was in Oaxaca, Mexico; and five African masks in a row staring down at me from the wall.

Iris comes back into the room holding a bamboo tray with two glasses of iced tea and what smells like fresh-baked lemon-snap cookies. She places the tray on a side table next to her chair and sits down. I take a cookie and a sip of some strange, unidentifiable tea and smile at her from across the antique mahogany wood table between us.

Crossing her legs, tucking her right foot under her left calf, she asks, "So, why are you here tonight?"

I have no idea what to say. I was expecting more foreplay, the usual back-and-forth between strangers.

"Don't you want to know where I'm from? People always start with that, and then I have to launch into my whole spiel. I was born in Stamford, Connecticut, moved to

Plantation, Florida, then to Atlanta, Georgia, then Tulsa, Oklahoma, then to Short Hills *and* Essex Fells, New Jersey, then Manhattan, Westchester, and back to Connecticut again. And no, I'm not an army brat." I inhale, smile, and wait for her to ask the standard follow-up question: "If you're not an army brat, then what are you?" I'm ready to respond with "corporate brat."

Iris's mood-ring eyes burrow into me, shifting from hazel to green. She leans forward, as if she's about to share a secret with me, and says, "Thank you, but I asked you why you're here tonight."

I laugh nervously.

"How long have you been doing this?" I ask.

"Kimberlee, I asked you a question."

I want to tell her to mind her own business and give me a break, I just got here, let me enjoy my cookie. But then it occurs to me that I'm paying this woman to help me . . . to help me with what? Why *am* I here tonight? It's not as simple as I want to get married and my boyfriend isn't ready. Or I hate my job. It's not as if I'm living on the streets or have some terminal disease. From the outside, I'm just another pretty white girl who seems to get along well in the world. But that's not how I feel inside. I don't know how to describe it. It's similar to that feeling you get when you've lost something valuable and sentimental, something you can't get back or replace, that pit in your stomach, the tingling in your arms, the regret you feel for not being able to remember the moment when it left you, not being able to go back in time. That's how I feel about my life. I feel lost and afraid, and all I want is for someone to tell me everything's going to be okay.

Iris is staring at me, waiting for me to say something.

I feel my face turn red.

"Okay," Iris says, her voice softening. "I'll ask another question. An easier one, perhaps. Why did you choose to see me?"

I clear my throat. "My friend Karen recommended you."

"Karen? Yes. Karen! A real sweetheart. A bright soul. A love."

Yes, Karen who tells me when Mercury is in retrograde. Karen who reminds me to check my Astrologyzone forecast on the first day of each month. And Karen who punches me in the arm every time she catches me Googling my boyfriend's ex-girlfriend.

"Karen is amazing. She's my savior at work," I say, pressing my hands to my chest the way old ladies do when they see babies. "I'd trust her with my life."

"I'm sorry to hear you work with her in that dungeon," Iris says.

Karen has obviously told her about our basement office at Fox News Channel and the twenty TV monitors that hang in a row on the wall in front of us, to our left and to our right, bombarding us with images of war and terror.

"Yeah. We both work on the Live Desk. I don't know if she told you that or not. We're responsible for producing breaking news for the channel and affiliate stations nationwide. We handle satellite space. We book fiber feeds, manage live shots, count down generics, update field producers with wire copy—"

"Stop," Iris says, lifting her hand. "I have no idea what you're talking about. Generics? You might as well be speaking another language."

"I'm sorry, I do that all the time. I lapse into industry speak without thinking. My boyfriend, Noah, thinks it's funny, but it's annoying, I know. Generics are live shots at the top of each hour that affiliate stations can take for free, as opposed to paying $125 for a five-minute custom live."

Iris shoots me a look.

"Sorry," I say, and smile. "Okay, let's say a reporter is covering wildfires in California. They'll get as close to the scene as possible and then update viewers on how many people have been killed, how many homes have been destroyed, that kind of thing, and then wrap with something like, 'I'm so and so, live from wherever in California for Fox News.' That's what we call a generic live. If a station wants to customize their shot, 'Back to you, Jim and Nancy, for Fox 25,' then they'll have to pay for it." I laugh and cover my face with my hands. "It's just so crazy to me that I've become the kind of person who knows all this, someone who can tell you the downlink frequency for IA6/K20D1," I say, shaking my head.

"What kind of person did you want to be?" Iris asks.

"Not someone who works at Fox, that's for sure. I've been there for almost eight years and I'm not even a technical person. Well, I guess I am. But it's not *who* I am, if you know what I mean."

"No. Tell me," Iris prods.

"Working at Fox is not why I'm here tonight, if that's what you're getting at. Yes, it's a toxic environment. People yelling. TVs blasting. Fifteen-minute lunch breaks. Gross, recycled air. No windows," I say, and count the windows in her living room. *One . . . two . . . three . . . four . . . five . . . six . . .*

"Windows are important," Iris declares. "Some say we're made of water. I say we're made of light."

Iris's business card pops into my head.

On the front, in light black letterpress print, it reads:

IRIS GOLDBLATT
TAROT READER
MIRROR OF THE SOUL
212-555-9043

On the back, in handwritten ballpoint cursive, it says:

Sitting quietly, doing nothing,
the flowers bloom effortlessly.

Maybe Iris is a fortune cookie incarnate.

"What did Karen tell you about me?"

"That you really helped her, that she loves you," I say, wondering how this woman is going to help me.

Iris lowers her glasses onto her nose to get an unmediated look at me. "Have you ever had your cards read?"

"No, but I've been to a Reiki Master, a craniosacral therapist, an intuitive acupuncturist, a hypnotherapist, and an astrologer named Rakesh. Oh, and another astrologer named Jimmy, but he wasn't very good."

"Well, you should know that I'm not your typical tarot reader. People often associate tarot with fortune-tellers and crystal balls. For good reason too. There are a lot of scam artists out there."

"I thought the cards were kind of like tea leaves, that you could read someone's future if you knew how to decode the shapes."

"I don't believe in reading the future."

Excuse me? A hot flush rushes up my arms, across my shoulders, down my back and legs into my feet. *But I need you to tell me my future. I need you to tell me that things are going to get better, that Noah and I are going to get married, have kids, be happy, that my life will amount to something, that I will finally become the person I am meant to be. That's why I'm here. That why I came to see you!* I feel myself getting smaller and smaller, my breath getting shorter and shorter. I'm spiraling. I'm a spiraler. That's what I do.

Iris snaps her fingers. "Wake up and close your eyes."

I stare at her unmoving.

prologue

"Come on, Kimberlee. Close your eyes."

I close my eyes, but open them a second later to see what she's doing. When I see that her eyes are closed too, I shut mine again and try to relax.

"Okay. Good. Breathe with me."

I take a breath and feel it stop in my chest.

"Breathe deep. Breathe into your diaphragm," Iris says, reminding me of my voice teacher at NYU, Pat Mullen, who would have us place our hands on our tummies and breathe so deep that our hands would push out with every breath. When I breathe deep, really deep, I cry, which is probably why I don't breathe deep.

I take another breath. It stops in my chest again.

"Take a breath in," Iris says, and breathes in.

"And breathe out," Iris says, and breathes out.

In.

Out.

In.

Out.

Before I know it, I'm breathing. Really breathing.

My chin starts to wobble.

Fuck. It's happening.

I hear Iris say, "Kimberlee, you need to take better care of yourself. You need more air. You need more water. You need more light."

I crack my eyes open and look at this strange woman sitting across from me and start to cry. I tilt my head back and wipe the corners of my eyes with my fingers to make sure my mascara doesn't run.

Unfazed, Iris hands me a Kleenex from her pocket and says, "Okay, Kimberlee. Let's begin. The cards will show us the way." She grabs the deck off the table and thumbs through it, pulling out cards as she goes. "Usually I use the whole deck, but tonight, I'm only going to use the Major Arcana."

I look at her as if she's channeling the spirit of Charlie Brown's teacher: *Whah, whah-whah, whaaah.*

"Major Arcana?"

"Yes, the tarot deck is comprised of seventy-eight cards: twenty-two Major Arcana, and fifty-six Minor Arcana or pip cards. The twenty-two Major Arcana cards hold the most meaning, the most significance, and have strong ties, not only to Jungian archetypes but also to the Kabbalah Tree of Life."

Talk about speaking another language.

"Can you please explain what that means?" I ask.

"In Lurianic Kabbalah, a sixteenth-century school of Jewish mysticism, it was understood that contemplating the sephirot—the ten emanations of the Tree of Life— could assist us in seeing the divine."

"All I know about Kabbalah is that Madonna and Ashton Kutcher are really into it."

Iris reaches under the table for a book and opens it to a picture of the Kabbalah Tree of Life.

"This is called the 'flash of lightning,'" Iris says, tracing her finger from top to bottom in a zigzag. "And this is 'the path of the serpent,'" she adds, zigzagging back up the tree. "All paths, ascending and descending, left to right, from Binah to Hesed, right to left, from Hesed to Hod,

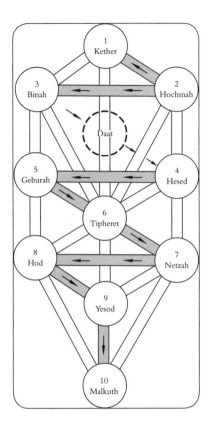

have meaning. They connect with the lessons of the Major Arcana. But this is not a Kabbalah lesson," she says, and closes the book.

"Phew," I say, and laugh.

"Tarot has a very real and long-standing spiritual and psychological base. For centuries, people have used these paths, symbols and archetypes to understand their humanity and divinity."

"Okeydokey."

"Kimberlee, if you're not serious about being here, you can leave."

"I'm sorry," I say. "I'm serious."

"I need to know that you are willing to explore new ways of seeing yourself and your life. I need you to be open with me. Open to this process. Can you do that?"

"Yes," I hear myself promising, worried I might fail by not understanding a word she says or not seeing something I'm supposed to see.

"There's no wrong way to do this. I just need your active participation. Are you ready?" Iris asks, her eyes turning sea-blue.

"Yes. I'm ready," I say, not at all ready.

She hands me the twenty-two whatever-they're-called and says, "Feel the energy of the cards, then put *your* energy into the cards by shuffling them as many times as you want. When you feel you have sufficiently charged the cards, hand them back to me."

I hold the thin stack of cards in my hands. *How do you shuffle twenty-two cards? What if I stop shuffling a second too soon? How will I know when my energy is in the cards?*

"Do what feels right," she says, placing her hand on top of my hand for a second.

My thoughts shut off like a lamp with her touch. I can actually feel the air in the room shift, like swimming into a warm spot in the ocean. I take a deep breath and feel my belly jut out over my jeans again, but I don't feel self-conscious or bad about it this time.

I shuffle once, twice, a third time and pause.

prologue

Three times seems so cliché.

I shuffle one more time and hold the cards tightly in my hands, trying to transmit all the hope in my heart through my fingertips.

"Okay, I think I'm ready," I say.

Iris cuts the deck with her right hand, the ruby ring on her middle finger sparkling like Mars in the night sky.

"Do you have the candle I asked you to bring?"

"The only one I could find was this green votive at the bodega around the corner," I say, pulling it out of my bag.

"That'll do."

She places the candle in a cobalt blue ceramic dish on the side table next to the tray of cookies and lights it with matches from Hell's Kitchen.

"That's my favorite restaurant! Don't you think it's some kind of sign I'm meant to be here?"

"I don't believe in signs. I believe we see what we want to see. They happen to have excellent guacamole. Are you ready?"

"Yes, I'm ready," I say, and this time I mean it.

THE FOOL.

El Loco / Le Bateleur
Arcana: 0
Path on Kabbalah Tree of Life: 11
Color: Pale Yellow
Planet: Uranus
Constellation: Cepheus
Musical note: E

the fool

> "If a man would persist in his folly,
> he would become wise."
> —WILLIAM BLAKE

Iris flips over the first card and places it in the center of the table. She puts the second one directly below the first, the third perpendicular to the second, the fourth above the first. The eleven cards, altogether, form the letter H. Iris studies the spread for what feels like ten minutes. I watch her eyes race back and forth and up and down. "Interesting," she says in a low mumble and looks back up at me.

What? What's so interesting?

She takes a sip of iced tea and leans back as if we were hanging out on a hot summer afternoon in rural Georgia instead of sitting in her living room at 10:20 P.M. on a Sunday night in New York City.

Come on! Tell me! What's so interesting?

The cards are upside down from where I'm sitting, except one. But I'm not wearing my glasses. And I can't make out the images. I lean in closer and see what looks like the Grim Reaper. "Omigod. I'm going to die?!"

"Of course, Kimberlee. We're all going to die."

"I know, but am I going to die soon?!"

"You have to be patient."

"I can't be patient. I'm totally freaked out."

"You get freaked out far too easily," Iris says as if she's known me for years.

I take a deep breath. *Calm down. Just calm down.*

"This is called the Grand Cross spread. A variation on the commonly used Celtic Cross spread. There are thousands of spreads. The Infinity spread. The Fifteen-Card Wish spread. The Astrological spread. The Kabbalah Tree of Life spread."

"Why did you choose this one?" I ask, taking another breath, my chest still tight.

"Intuition," she says with the certainty of a scientist.

"But I thought you said you weren't psychic."

"I said no such thing. I said I do not believe in reading the future. Two different things," she says, and looks at me as if I'm crazy for confusing the two.

"So you *are* psychic?"

"It doesn't matter what *I* am. It matters what *you* are. What *you* see."

"So you could tell me my future, but you're choosing not to?"

"You're missing the point."

I adjust my legs and feel my jeans stick to my skin. Even with all the windows open, her apartment is still hot.

"This is your self card," Iris continues, handing it to me. "Each card's placement has significance. This card, in this position, represents *you* at the time of the reading. And in your case, it's the Fool."

"The Fool?!" I say, my eyebrows shooting straight up. "So, wait. I'm the Fool? *I'm* the Fool?"

"Does that resonate for you?" Iris asks.

"Well . . . I mean, I guess. I just turned thirty-three and definitely feel like there's some owner's manual to life I never got."

"What does that mean?"

"I don't know how to explain it really. Three of my girlfriends took me out to dinner for my birthday. They got me flowers. They were totally nice. But as I sat across from them sipping sauvignon blanc and eating edamame, I felt like they had figured out this life thing and left me behind somehow."

"In what way?"

"They're all married. One of them is pregnant. The other two are thinking about trying to conceive. They all make well over six figures and feel creatively fulfilled in their jobs. They were talking about how difficult it is for a woman to have it all. And there I was, no husband, no kids, no real career to speak of. It just made me feel like shit—sorry, I try not to curse. When I was twelve, my father overhead me say the 'f' word, threw me against the sliding glass door in the kitchen and screamed, 'Women shouldn't curse.' His fist was shaking with such rage he accidentally hit my mouth. I had a fat lip for a week."

"No," Iris says, horrified. "Did he do that kind of thing often?"

"No, no. He had a bad temper and yelled a lot, but no, he never hit us. He just thought women who cursed sounded like truck drivers."

"Well, you don't sound like a truck driver to me," Iris says, and gently touches my knee. "You sound like someone who is very hard on herself."

"Everyone's hard on me. My friends. My family. They all keep grilling me. 'Why isn't Noah ready to get married?' 'Why don't you give him an ultimatum?' 'Why are you still in a job you don't like?' "

"So you're getting a lot of outside pressure."

"Outside pressure is an understatement."

"How long have you and Noah been together?"

"We just celebrated our third-year anniversary."

"And do you want to marry Noah?"

"Yes, and it was terrible because on our anniversary, he handed me a little black box and I thought he was proposing and then I opened the box and inside were ruby earrings. I know, so sweet, but I felt like such an idiot. I was like, 'Oh, earrings. Thanks,'" I say, imitating my forced smile.

"I think you might be misinterpreting the Fool. It is actually the most spiritual card in the deck. In the Kabbalah Tree of Life, the Fool is placed outside the tree. He is the divine point of entry. Endless and unknowable. Transcendent. In Hebrew he translates into: *Ain*, meaning 'no thing'; *Ain Sof*, meaning 'absolute all'; and *Ain Sof Aur*, meaning 'limitless light.' We're all fools on this journey of life. The fact that the Fool is reversed in your spread gives me a better idea of why you're here."

"Reversed?"

"It means you're having a hard time learning the lesson associated with this card."

I exhale hard, the air rushing out of my mouth fast, causing my lips to jut out and vibrate like a horse's lips.

"What do you see when you look at the card?" Iris asks.

"Um, a man in tights? All of his possessions in a sack on a stick swung over his shoulder. If he takes one more step, he's going to fall off that cliff and die."

"That's all very true, but what does it mean to you?"

"It means nothing to me. It's just a guy on a card."

"What do you think he's trying to teach you?"

"I don't know."

"Look again," Iris commands.

I look more closely. I study his outfit and try to find meaning in the colors. I look at the flower, the dog, the sky, the cliff. *The Fool . . . a fool . . . a fool in love . . . to be made a fool. Come on, Kimberlee. You can do this. The Fool . . . a dreamer . . . oblivious to his surroundings . . . about to fall off a cliff . . .*

★ ★ ★

Short Hills, New Jersey, was the cool capital of the world, and I was the weird transplant from Bumble-fuck, Oklahoma, who wore plaid blazers and shook everyone's hand with a smile: "Hi, my name is Kimberlee Auerbach, nice to meet you."

"Nice to meet you" didn't fly with the sixth graders at Deerfield Elementary School. They had all sorts of secret handshakes involving knuckle smacking and finger snapping. The girls wore heavy blue eyeliner, ripped jeans and scissor-cut sweatshirts that hung off one shoulder à la *Flash-dance*. Some of them even went to second base on the jungle gym during recess. I couldn't imagine kissing a boy, let alone letting him feel my boob.

I wished my popularity in Tulsa had automatically transferred over, like some universal cool pass that said: "Kimberlee Auerbach had fifteen awesome friends before, so be nice to her."

But no, I was the dorky new girl who had to pay her dues and learn new rules. Ironed Wrangler jeans: not cool. White E.G. Smith socks: cool. Red silk ribbons tied around your head in a bow: not cool. Perms: cool. Having a crush on Ted Weiner: not cool. French-kissing Josh Kahn: cool.

Josh was the coolest kid in school. He looked like John Belushi, only smaller. He even wore the same black sunglasses.

I didn't think he knew who I was, but then one day, during recess, he walked over to me and said, "Hi, Kim," as if he said my name all the time.

I was sitting by myself on the playground asphalt eating an apple.

He squatted down in front of me, extending his arm out, fist closed. My heart started to do somersaults. Was he giving me a Blow Pop ring? Asking me out? He opened his hand slowly. Resting in the middle of his palm was a dingy gray screw. Choking on laughter, barely able to get the words out, he asked, "Wanna screw?"

I looked behind him, and saw that his friends were cracking up too. I wanted to hide under a rock.

When I got home from school, I begged my mother to buy me a pink NAFNAF jumpsuit with silver studs and fifteen black rubber bracelets. No more Sandra Dee. I was going to be a Pink Lady!

By the time sixth graded ended, I was no longer a dork. I was about to move up to Milburn Junior High for seventh grade and I was ready.

On my first day of school, I walked through the double doors of the massive brick building, wearing a fluorescent-paint-splattered Esprit T-shirt and matching orange nail polish. Instead of shaking people's hands, I smiled at everyone I passed in the hallways and nodded my head as if I were already part of some secret society.

Later that morning, three girls sat next to me in science class. Jenny had freckles. Alison had Brooke Shields eyebrows. And Sarah had the bluest eyes I had ever seen.

Somehow, looking at amoebas under a microscope turned into making plans to see *Ghostbusters* at the Milburn movie theater. It was easy. They just seemed to like me. Or maybe they liked my outfit. I wasn't sure and I didn't care.

After school, I bounded off the bus and into the kitchen, where my mother stood at the sink cleaning asparagus. Snap. Snap. Snap. She had taught me the importance of snapping off the ends at their natural breaking point. Her blond hair was sparkling in the afternoon light along with her gold ram's head bracelet, Cartier watch, diamond ring, sapphire and ruby ring and an ancient coin pendant surrounded by diamonds dangling at the end of a long gold chain.

"Kimmi! How did it go?" she asked me, her smile as wide as the sun.

"Mom, I made three new friends! Jenny, Alison and Sarah."

"That's wonderful!" She dropped the asparagus into the colander and hugged me, her wet hands soaking the back of my shirt. Our chocolate brown poodle, Chloe, was barking in the background and our green parrot, Fred, was saying his own name over and over, "Hello, Freeeeeeed. Hello, Freeeeeeed."

My younger brother, Michael, rushed in and asked, "What's going on?"

I didn't have the heart to tell him about my new friends and I didn't have the stomach to hear about how mean the kids at school were to him, how Jason Steinman called him "tumor boy" as he had the year before—although his face did look less puffy today. Michael was three years behind me in school, so he had to go to Deerfield Elementary, where he was still the new kid, and still the kid with tumors. I patted him on the head and asked if he wanted to play Donkey Kong downstairs.

When dinner was ready, my mother yelled at us from the top of the stairs, "Soup's on, girls and boys!" My father was running late, so we sat down and started without him. Grilled chicken and a side of steamed asparagus, an Auerbach standard. I preferred taco night, but I could wait three days.

Twenty minutes later, the sound of a car pulling into the driveway catapulted us to our feet. "Dad's home," we all yelled, and ran to the door.

My father was like a guest celebrity, making special appearances.

He put his briefcase down and kissed all of us on the head, my mother included. We trailed behind him and took our seats. My father sat at the head of the table, loosening his tie and exhaling like a king, his protruding stomach hitting the table lip. We waited for my mother to serve him before we dove back in.

"How was your day, honey?" my mother asked.

"Fine, darling. Just fine."

We all sighed with collective relief.

"Kimma. Thirteen plus four?" my father asked.

My brother started laughing. My father and brother had bonded over current events and numbers, both of which I hated.

I counted with my fingers under the table. "Seventeen?" I said.

"Bravo! You get three points."

I had no idea if these points were being tallied somewhere or for what kind of prize. I just smiled and hoped there weren't more questions.

"Name a continent," he continued.

My brother laughed again, and my mother tried to protect me: "Mark . . ."

"Name a continent," he repeated.

"China," I said.

"Wrong! Minus three points."

I was no longer happy that my father had come home. I looked over at my brother, who was scratching his scar. It was hard to look at. Most of the time though, I didn't notice.

"May I be excused?" I asked.

"After you clear the table and clean the dishes," my mother said.

My brother never had to clean the dishes. He was the prince of the family and got to go downstairs and watch *Family Ties*.

The next morning, I woke up to my pink Swatch alarm clock's Muzak version of "Here Comes the Sun." I put on leggings with stirrups and an oversized blue and white Benetton rugby and ran downstairs to eat breakfast. My mother poured skim milk into my bowl of Cheerios, and then sat down to eat her oatmeal. When she finished, she brought her bowl to the sink and grabbed paper towels to clean Fred's cage. As soon as she opened the cage door, he flew out. His wings were clipped, but he could still fly short distances. I looked over my shoulder and saw he was heading toward me. I tried to move, but it was too late. He made a crash landing in my Cheerios. I pushed back in my chair and watched him flap around in the milk. My brother and I couldn't stop laughing. Then Fred flew onto my shoulder and took a dump.

"MOM!" I screamed.

My mother ran over, grabbed Fred and put him back in the cage. "Jesus, Fred!" She waved her finger at him. "Bad boy, Fred. Bad, bad boy."

My favorite shirt was now covered in milk and parrot poop. I ran upstairs and changed into another shirt, not as cute, but it matched my leggings. I sprinted out front just as the bus arrived. I found a seat in the back and stared out the window. "Sister Christian" was playing in my head, but just the refrain. I didn't know all the words. I couldn't believe it; I was actually excited to go to school.

Walking to homeroom on my second day, I spotted Alison. The old Kimmi would have run up to her and squealed. But cool girls don't squeal. I let her come to me. She leaned in and kissed me hello on the cheek. It was worth suffering sixth grade for this moment.

"Hey, did you read about the election?" she asked.

"No."

"Well, I'm thinking of running for president. You should run for vice president. It would be sooo much fun."

"Sounds great," I said with a cool confidence that surprised me.

The bell rang and we scurried off to our homerooms. Everything was falling into place. I loved my new friends. I loved my classes. I even raised my hand in Social Studies to offer my opinion on propaganda, which was something along the lines of "Propaganda is bad."

After school, I rushed into the house screaming at the top of my lungs, "Mom, you're never going to believe it!"

"What Kimmi? What happened?" my mother screamed from the top of the staircase. Her hair was wet and she was holding an eyelash curler. I had forgotten my parents were going to a charity event in the city.

"I decided to run for vice president of my class," I said, and ran up the stairs.

"Oh God, I thought something was wrong," she said. My mother was always bracing herself for bad news. You'd never know it if you weren't related to her. She smiled when she wasn't happy and her voice was as sweet and airy as cotton candy. "Vice president? Wow. That's wonderful," she said, squeezing me hard, tears pooling in her eyes. That was another thing about my mother. She cried. At weddings. At rainbows. At commercials. And sometimes she cried in the bathroom with the door locked so my father couldn't get to her.

"Mom, it's okay," I said, patting her on the back.

"I know. I know. I'm just so proud of you." She wiped her eyes, grabbed both my shoulders and looked into my eyes. "We are going to win this race!"

With my mother it was always "we," and I loved it.

The next morning, I put on my mint green cotton miniskirt and matching cardigan. I didn't have the luxury of another top that would match, so I asked my mother to wait until after I left to clean Fred's cage.

"Kimmi, I dreamt of the perfect slogan for you last night," she said, standing at the kitchen counter, grinding coffee beans.

"Really?!"

She stopped what she was doing, threw her hands up in the air as if she were painting the words in lights, and said, "Don't Dance Around the Issues. Vote Kim Auerbach for Vice President. She Bops!"

"Mom! That is sooooo coooool. I love it!"

She grabbed my hands and twirled me around. The bus wouldn't be here for another ten minutes, so she shimmied over to the bookcase, pulled her favorite record out of its case, slid it onto the silver spindle and gently placed the needle down.

You better knock, on wood, baby.

"Ooooooooh, ooooo, ooooo, ooooo, ooooo, oooooooh," we sang along.

My brother joined in and the three of us danced our brains out. My father was still upstairs, probably using his tortoiseshell shoehorn to get his Italian leather loafers on or trying to figure out which cufflinks to wear.

When the song was over, my mother shuffled us outside to catch the bus. I wondered if she'd keep dancing or if my father would find some reason to yell at her.

During lunch, I signed up for the election and ran over to the table where Jenny, Alison and Sarah were eating.

"It's official," I said, placing my hand on my hip.

Alison gave me high five and offered me a bite of her Sloppy Joe. I was too excited to eat.

After school, my mother drove me to the store to get art supplies so I could make my posters. I got fifteen poster boards, five glitter glue sticks and a packet of multicolored Magic Markers.

When we got home, I locked myself in my bedroom, turned on the radio and started on the first poster. In big red bubble letters I wrote, "Don't Dance Around the Issues. Vote Kim Auerbach for Vice President. She Bops!" In the bottom-right-hand corner, I drew a picture of Cyndi Lauper wearing a top hat, holding a cane. Then I put glitter around the edges for a dramatic effect.

One down, fourteen to go.

Every day when I came home from school, I worked on my posters. After a week, I was finally finished. I announced my accomplishment with a scream from my bedroom, "Mom, I'm done!"

A few minutes later, she opened my bedroom door and flashed her Revlon frosted-pink lipstick smile. "Oh, Kimmi, they're just beautiful. Ready for the world to see them?"

"Ready!"

the fool

It was a quiet Sunday afternoon, Captain Black tobacco smoke wafting through the air, smelling of vanilla and bark. My father was in the living room, puffing away on his pipe, buried in the paper. My brother, a severe asthmatic, was playing Pac-Man downstairs.

My mother drove me to school and helped me find an open door. Together, we hung the posters all over: the library, the hallways and all four walls of the cafeteria. We were partners in crime. I was lucky to have my mother as my best friend. When we finished we looked at each other and said in unison, "Ice cream." We nodded and headed to Carvel.

Before going to bed that night, I took out my Magic 8 Ball, closed my eyes and shook it hard. "Will I be the next vice president of the seventh grade?" I asked aloud. I opened my eyes and watched the triangular die swirl around in the dark green-black liquid until it made its way to the top. The letters slowly came into focus: *It is decidedly so.*

All night, I dreamt of horses and first-place ribbons and kids walking through the hallways at school, stopping me along the way, patting me on the shoulder to congratulate me.

"Here Comes the Sun" woke me up at 7 A.M. as it did any other day. But this wasn't any other day. This was *my* day.

I walked into school in my pink NAFNAF jumpsuit with the silver studs, and just as in my dream, kids were coming up to me—seventh graders and eighth graders alike—patting me on the shoulder, saying, "Good one." I was making a real name for myself. I was going to be vice president of my seventh-grade class. I could feel it. Life couldn't get better than this.

In homeroom, I sat down in my usual seat behind Wendy Rostein, a Goth girl who wore black lipstick and a dog collar and never spoke to me.

She turned around and asked me, "Do you even know what 'She Bops' means?"

"Yeah, it means to dance in, like, a really cool way."

"Uh, no. It means you masturbate," she said, and laughed.

I didn't know what masturbate meant, but I knew it couldn't be good. I felt sick to my stomach, so I excused myself to the nurse's office.

As I ran through the hallways, I tried not to catch anyone's eye. But a group of older boys standing by the lockers blocked me. "Hey there, Kim Auerbach. Where ya going so fast? Are you off to 'Bop'?!" Then they started singing, "She bop, he-bop-a-we-bop, I bop, you-bop-a-they-bop, be bop, be-bop-a-lu, she bop."

The nurse called my mother, who sped over to pick me up.

"Kimmi, what's wrong?" she asked as I crawled into the front seat. My mother wasn't used to seeing me cry. She reached over to hug me.

"Don't touch me. You ruined my life."

"Excuse me?"

"'She Bops' means 'she masturbates'!"

"Oh, sweetie, honey, I'm so sorry, I didn't know that. I thought it meant to dance in, like, a really cool way."

"Yeah, that's what I thought too," I said.

When we got home, I ran upstairs and locked myself in my room. I didn't even come down for dinner. I threw my glitter pens in my wicker trash bin, crawled under my pink and white striped Laura Ashley sheets and turned on the radio. I wanted to hear Prince's "When Doves Cry," but Cyndi Lauper's "Time After Time" was playing. The Universe was laughing at me. I hated everything and everyone.

My brother slipped a note under my door that said, "Kimmi, I'm sorry you're sad," and then my mother knocked on my door at around 9 P.M.

"You can't come in," I yelled.

She opened the door, walked over to me and sat down on the bed.

"Kimmi, I know this is hard for you," she said, stroking my hair.

"Mom?"

"Yes, Kimmi?"

"What does masturbate mean?"

"Well, Kimmi . . ."

"It's really bad, isn't it?"

"No, it's not bad. It's when . . . it's when you touch your vagina. It's not polite to do in public, and it's important to wash your hands afterward. But sweetie, there's nothing wrong with masturbating."

I pulled the covers over my head. The thought of everyone in school picturing me touching my vagina made me want to move to Alaska.

31

"When we touch ourselves or *invite* someone else to touch us, it's perfectly fine. It's more than fine. I never *ever* want you to feel ashamed or dirty, the way I was made to feel as a kid. Our bodies are natural. Sex is natural. Those kids can shove it." She kissed me on the forehead. "Now try to get some sleep, angel baby."

On her way out, she whispered "sweet dreams" and then shut the door.

I didn't have sweet dreams that night and I didn't win the race. Stephanie Green did. But that was okay. She was my new friend. I had lots of new friends. The whole "She Bops" thing actually ended up working in my favor. I may have lost, but I was no loser. Kids now thought of me as sexually advanced. Apparently touching your vagina is cooler than being vice president.

★   ★   ★

"What does the Fool mean to me?" I repeat back to Iris. "Well, he's all la-di-da, about to fall off a cliff and die. Totally clueless. Not paying attention to the dog trying to warn him. I feel like this card is telling me I'm not paying attention to something I should be paying attention to. I worry about that a lot. I'm afraid of being a fool."

"The Fool is innocent, unaware of danger or consequence, that is true. But I don't think it means you're not paying attention to something. I think it's more about control with you," Iris says.

"Control?"

"Yes. C-o-n-t-r-o-l," Iris says, her voice dropping even deeper than usual.

"You don't need to spell it out for me."

"Isn't that exactly what you want me to do? Listen, Kimberlee. You have trouble breathing. You worry too much. You focus on the wrong things," Iris says, tucking a flyaway strand of silver hair behind her ear. "You think if you do this, if you do that, then you'll be able to control the outcome. You'll be able to protect yourself from hurt and embarrassment. But we can never foresee the hurt in our lives."

"But don't you think you can make better choices than others?"

"The more experience we have, the better choices we can make."

"I just feel like I don't know how to choose right anymore. I've made some serious mistakes in the past. Really bad choices. I've picked the wrong men. The wrong food. The wrong job. Now everyone is telling me to break up with Noah. . . . I just really don't want to get hurt again. What's wrong with that?"

"Nothing's wro—"

"Is the Fool trying to tell me I will get hurt, no matter what?"

"Kimberlee, there are no guarantees in life. You could marry Noah and get divorced. Happens all the time. That is what the Fool is trying to tell you."

"That Noah and I are going to get divorced?"

"You're a funny girl," Iris says, shaking her head. "The Fool represents living in the moment. If we spend our whole lives holding on too tight, afraid of doing it wrong, afraid of what we might lose, then we'll miss out on so much beauty, so much life. Be the Fool, Kimberlee. Embrace it. There are far worse things to be."

WHEEL of FORTUNE.

La Rueda De La Fortuna / La Roue De La Fortune
Arcana: X
Path on Kabbalah Tree of Life: 21
Color: Violet
Planet: Jupiter
Constellation: Capricornus
Musical note: A Sharp

wheel of fortune

"Everything goes, everything returns,
eternally rolls the wheel of being."
—FRIEDRICH NIETZSCHE

With a smirk on her face, Iris hands me the next card. Her impishness is surprising for someone so old. Well, maybe not so old. In this light, she looks forty. Maybe fifty. Her face is dewy and barely lined. "How old are you?" I ask, staring at her face, avoiding the card in my hand.

"Didn't your mother teach you better?"

"I'm sorry. I didn't mean to offend you. Really. I think you look good. You're a beautiful woman."

Iris uncrosses her arms and looks me up and down. "Thank you. You're rather fetching yourself. How old do you think I am?"

How old do you think I am? is always a trap. If I guess right, she won't be happy. If I guess too old, she definitely won't be happy. If I guess too young, she'll think I'm trying to flatter her.

"Your silver hair is throwing me off. Your face . . . Late forties? Early fifties?"

"Sixty-six," she says, and smiles.

"Are you serious?! You look fantastic. I mean, you looked good before. But sixty-six? Wow."

"We all get older. It's part of life. Stages. Cycles. Seasons. Which actually brings us to your next card," she says, pointing down at my hand.

My eyes remain fixed on her face as I fiddle with the dull edges of the card.

"Kimberlee, please."

I peer down and see *Wheel of Fortune* written in black, bold print at the bottom.

"And the seasons, they go round and round," Iris starts to sing.

There's a red creature rising, a yellow snake slithering and a dude with an Egyptian headdress about to fall off a wheel.

"What's with all the falling?" I ask Iris.

"Round and round and round in the circle game," Iris continues.

"Are you saying *this* has something to do with Joni Mitchell?" I ask.

"Is that what I'm saying? I thought I was singing. Come on, Kimberlee. Look at the card."

"I am looking at the card. This blue guy," I say, and point. "He's about to fall off the wheel."

"What else?" Iris asks.

"I don't know. There's some kind of winged creature in each corner and they're all reading blank books. I'm a blank slate? Is that it?"

"You don't look like tabula rasa to me," Iris says, and winks.

"I got nothing," I say, and hand her back the card.

"Don't give up," she says, refusing to take it.

"What do you want me to see?" I ask.

"Sometimes we are on top. Other times we are on bottom. It's the nature of life. It's cyclical. Always moving. Never stagnant."

"I don't understand how that relates to my life or what's been going on."

"And what exactly has been going on? Aside from the fact that you're jealous of your friends and Noah gave you ruby earrings instead of proposing."

*   *   *

From: Dad
Subject: Dinner
To: Kimmi
Dinner? 6:30? Steak? Love ya
Sent via BlackBerry from Cingular Wireless

the devil, the lovers, & me

From: Kimmi
Subject: Re: Dinner
To: Dad
Steak sounds good. I like steak. Tell me where and I'll be there.
I love you, Kimmi

Whenever my father comes to the city, I change my plans to see him. An old acting teacher once told me that if someone really wants an orange, he will accept one slice of orange over an entire apple. I've been living on slices with my dad my whole life.

I walked into Morton's Steakhouse at 6:30 P.M. sharp and asked the boob-job hostess if my father had arrived. "The name is Auerbach," I said, trying not to look at her cleavage as she bent down and checked the reservation. She smiled and pointed to my father sitting at a table toward the back, facing the front door like a Mafia don.

He was in the middle of asking the waiter about the wines on the list. I suspected he saw me approaching, but he continued talking to the waiter: "Is this as big as the Barolo?" When the waiter said yes, my father gave him the nod, as if assigning a hit, and then looked at me.

"Kimma! How are ya?" he said, opening his arms in his shtick-y way.

I don't know why he calls me Kimma. It makes me feel fat.

I kissed him on the cheek and sat down, placing my

purse on the shoulder of the chair and wiggling in the seat to get comfortable. I was nervous. I never knew what to say.

When I was in my early twenties, I got a job as a cigar girl at Decade, on the Upper East Side. My father loved cigars at the time. He had three humidors at home and more in his office. I figured if I studied the history of cigars, if I knew what they tasted like, if I knew the various brands, then we would have something to talk about. But after two nights of walking around the crowded club, carrying a silver tray of smelly, brown penis-looking things, having men gawk at me, call me "sweet tits" and grab my ass, I quit. My father was disappointed in me. "You care too much about what other people think," he said. So what if I knew the difference between a Romeo y Julieta and an Arturo Fuente? All he saw when he looked at me was my weakness.

The waiter poured my father a taste of wine. My father swirled, sniffed, sipped and then nodded his head in approval. The waiter took his cue and filled my glass and then his. My father stared at me, waiting to see what I thought of the wine.

"It's delicious," I said, not sure of the proper adjectives to use to describe a wine that was "as big as the Barolo."

He smiled.

For a man who acts as if he's above everyone else, he sure likes approval.

"So?" he asked.

"So?" I asked, not liking the dangerous and agenda-filled look in his eyes.

"I've been thinking about it," he said. "And it's time for Noah to propose."

"Excuse me?" I said, my red wine going up my nose.

"At some point, it's just insulting. If he won't commit, he's using you," he said, and then bent down, pulling out a plastic bag from his briefcase. "I hope you can learn something from this," he said, and slid the bag across the table toward me.

I reached in and pulled out a book: *Closing the Deal: Two Married Guys Take You from Single Miss to Wedded Bliss.*

"I saw them on CBS's morning show," he said. "They were talking about how to get a man to marry you. I thought to myself, *I gotta get Kimma this book!* So I went to Barnes and Noble, told the information guy I was looking for a book. He handed me *He's Just Not That into You.* 'No, that's not the problem,' I told him. He pointed me downstairs to the relationship section. You wouldn't believe how many *fakacta* relationship books there are. I started to walk back up the stairs, and guess what? I saw the book on display! Just like that! There it was."

"Dad, I know you mean well, but please," I begged in a whisper.

"It's insulting. You're a beautiful woman. Why should you wait around for a man? You don't need to wait for a man."

"Dad, I don't want to get married for the sake of being married."

"Don't give me that malarkey," he said, his face turning red.

42

I wanted to point out that he was on his fourth marriage and should shut up, but I took a deep breath and said, "I want to marry Noah. Yes. We're working on it. Dad, he's very good to me. Isn't that enough?"

"He is good to you. I actually think Noah would make an excellent life partner, but he has to step up to the plate," he said, pulling a piece of bread out of the basket. "Frankly, I think if you broke up with him, he would come back with a ring."

"I can't break up with Noah as some ploy, Dad."

"Are you guys ready to order?" the waiter asked.

"Yes, I'll have the iceberg salad with blue cheese dressing and the filet mignon very rare. Very rare," my father said, hitting the table with the tops of his chubby fingers to make a point.

"Black and blue, it is, sir," the waiter said, knowing my father's type. "And you?" the waiter turned to me and asked.

"Uh," I said, flipping the book over so he couldn't read the title. "I'll have the salmon with spinach."

"Good choice," he said, and walked away.

"Listen, Kimma. I promise I'll never bring it up again, but last week . . . ," he said, reaching back into his briefcase.

Oh God! Not another book.

"Last week I was at my jeweler getting one of my watches fixed and saw the most beautiful antique diamond ring and thought, *This is my daughter's engagement ring!*"

He opened the bag and took out a black velvet box.

I gasped.

"Tell Noah he can buy it from me whenever he's ready. It's a special ring, like no other. Just like my daughter."

OH MY FUCKING GOD! MY FATHER JUST PRO-POSED TO ME!

My face felt hot, and the smell of charcoal-grilled meat wafting through the air was making me sick. I turned away so I couldn't glimpse the ring, and excused myself to the ladies' room.

I slipped outside to catch my breath instead.

As I stood in front of the restaurant, practically hyperventilating, a tall man with dark hair and a kind face walked over to me. Maybe he could be my husband. Maybe he would want to marry me. Maybe he thought I needed the Heimlich.

He asked me if I had a light.

"I'm sorry. I don't smoke," I said. I wished I smoked. I wished there were something in my life that could give me instant comfort. I wanted to call Noah; he was my real comfort. But I couldn't call Noah. I couldn't tell him that my father had gotten me an engagement ring.

I took a deep breath and headed back inside.

I didn't want my father to know he had gotten to me, so I ducked into the ladies' room to splash water on my face. I walked over to the sink and looked at myself in the mirror, noticing everything wrong: the pimple on my forehead, my bloodshot eyes, my belly. I wiped the black liner from underneath my eyes and adjusted my skirt—the zipper had somehow inched its way over to the front where it didn't belong.

As I approached my father, I counted the seconds to see how long it would take for him to look up from his Black-Berry.

Thirty.

"Where were you?" he asked, continuing to type an email.

"Sorry, I had to make a call."

For the rest of the evening, we made small talk and ate like normal people. He told me about his purebred white Coton dog and how he likes to curl up on his pillow at night, and how in thunderstorms he gets so freaked out that he actually sleeps on my father's head. I kept my eyes on my mashed potatoes and said, "Wow, that's cool," in a monotone voice.

I looked up briefly at one point and saw my father chomping on his salad. His mouth was open and he had blue cheese dressing all over his chin. I was pretty sure he had on the most expensive watch in the room, but inside, he was still a poor Jewish boy from the Bronx.

After we finished our entrées, he asked me if I wanted dessert. I shook my head no, so he asked for the check. As he was signing the bill, he joked, "Do you think people think you're my daughter or girlfriend?" *Ew.* I looked at the family sitting next to us, eating their creamed spinach in peace, and hoped they didn't just hear that.

As we stood in front of the restaurant in awkward silence, he handed me a twenty for a cab. I thanked him. He patted me on the back with one hand and walked away.

I know he loves me. I know he loves me. I know he loves me.

This is what I keep telling myself about the men in my life.

*   *   *

"My father got me an engagement ring," I say to Iris, leaving out the night's gory details. "Well, he got it for Noah to give me."

"That's some father you have," Iris says, and laughs.

"Yeah, he's something," I say, rolling my eyes back, catching a glimpse of the sky mural painted on the ceiling.

"Do you know the difference between psychology and sociology?" Iris asks.

Talk about a non sequitur.

"I like to describe it this way," she says. "Let's say we didn't know about the seasons. We might see a leaf fall to the ground and wonder why. Look! A squirrel jumped on that branch over there and that orange leaf fell. But if we stepped back, we might notice something bigger happening. Lots of leaves are falling. It's a trend. It's a cycle. It's autumn. And it has nothing to do with a silly squirrel."

"What does that have to do with my father?"

"It doesn't. It has to do with you. I think you're stuck on the wheel, fixated on one particular point, instead of seeing the larger picture. Our lives are like the seasons. Sometimes we are on top. Other times we are on the bottom. If we remain grounded throughout life's ups and downs, we won't be as easily knocked around and damaged."

*   *   *

One rainy Saturday afternoon in 1985, my father took me shopping at the Short Hills Mall. As we entered Bloomingdale's, he noticed that everything I pulled from the racks was color coordinated. My socks had to match my shirt had to match my scrunchie. He was the CEO of Keystone Camera Corporation at the time and, on that particular Saturday, he realized there was a hole in the market. No one had come out with a camera you could wear, a camera you could match with your outfit.

Camera as accessory. It was genius. And I was the inspiration.

A year later, Le Clic cameras, the multicolored plastic disc cameras that took off in the 80s, were born. And I became the "Le Clic girl." I went from being the most teased girl in sixth grade to the most talked-about girl in seventh grade to gracing the pages of *Seventeen*, *Vogue* and *Elle* magazines in eighth, ninth and tenth grades. Limos picked me up from school in the middle of the day to take me to New York City for photo shoots, and practically every other weekend we had a black-tie event to attend. We flew Concorde to London, where I made in-store appearances at Harrods. We traveled to Cologne, Germany, for photokina, the world's largest photo trade show, where I pretended to be a mannequin in front of our booth wearing a Le Clic sweatshirt and bright red leggings. I even got to dance around in a commercial with Matt LeBlanc before he became famous on *Friends*. From the outside, my life seemed exciting and glamorous—every girl's dream.

But it had a dark side.

Juniors and seniors at Newark Academy (the private school my parents sent me to after seventh grade) said mean things behind my back. "The only reason she's a model is because of her dad." "She's too fat to be a model." "She's not even that pretty." And then I would be on a shoot in New York City with "real" models and overhear the makeup artist say to the photographer, "CEO's daughter." I didn't know what to think of myself. Was I pretty? Was I fat? The boys my age wouldn't come near me, and my father's business partners couldn't keep their eyes off me. I just wanted to be a normal teenaged girl with a cute boyfriend who listened to Pink Floyd and tried to get to third base in the backseat of his car.

When the stock market crashed in 1987, it looked as if I might get the chance to be normal.

But it wasn't over.

Not yet.

My father was in the process of selling Mitsubishi the rights to distribute Le Clic cameras in Japan as a last-ditch effort to save the company. To close the deal, he planned a ten-day trip to Tokyo, and since I was the Le Clic girl, it made sense to bring me along.

I was sixteen years old and had never spent that kind of time with my father. What would we talk about? What would we do? I had to prepare. I tried to read Nietzsche, my dad's favorite philosopher. I learned the difference between Noh and Kabuki theater, in case it came up in conversation. And I knew how to say *Ko-ni-chi-wa O-gen-ki-dis-ka?* ("Hello, how are you?")

Turned out, I was fairly inconsequential to the trip, just eye candy.

I spent my days with the escort my father got me, a young woman named Keiko who had a big head, smooth skin and jet-black hair that she wore in a ponytail. We didn't have much in common, other than our love for black and white stripes and sweet iced coffee from vending machines. At least with Keiko, I knew I wouldn't have to worry about being quizzed. I was pretty sure I couldn't have had an intelligent conversation about Nietzsche anyway.

Keiko took me to gardens and museums and restaurants during the day, and then at around 5 P.M. she would drop me off at the Ana Hotel Tokyo so I could get ready for dinner. Women generally weren't allowed to attend dinners with men, especially business dinners, but being "the daughter" and the Le Clic girl, I got to tag along.

I hopped in the shower on our last evening, dried myself off with the fluffiest white towel I had ever seen and stood in front of the mirror naked while I put on my makeup. No one had ever seen me naked, now that I had breasts and pubic hair. All of my friends had given hand jobs; some had even lost their virginity. Not me. I had kissed two boys, and I often wondered what it would be like to be fingered.

I poured a dime-sized dot of Christian Dior foundation into my palm and blended it into my skin in dabs. I brushed my cheekbones with dusty pink Clinique rouge. I licked the top of a Q-tip and dipped it into navy blue eye shadow; it created a smoky look. I curled my eyelashes and piled on dark black mascara. Then I swiped Chanel Paris

Pink lipstick across my lips. My mother had taught me well. After finishing my makeup ritual, I slipped on my bra, underwear, stockings, and a forest green dress with puffy sleeves, and matching leather heels.

My father and the men were waiting for me in the lobby. When they saw me, they stood up and bowed. My dad was beaming.

Dinner was my choice that night. We had already been to Tokyo's best French restaurant. We had eaten Italian. We had had fresh fish. I wanted Benihana.

When we walked into the restaurant, I was expecting to see communal tables, wooden bars, people laughing, making a ruckus. But this place was nothing like the chain restaurant near the Short Hills Mall. It was dark and everyone was whispering.

An older Japanese man wearing a black jacket escorted the seven of us to a private room. Inside, there was a rectangular table with an enormous grill in the center. We sat down in sort of a horseshoe shape. I was in the center, surrounded by men like a pearl pendant on a necklace.

The chef came in and stood directly across from me. His oily skin was shiny in the light. He smiled, bowed and then reached into a bucket next to him. "Yu lika shimp?"

I nodded.

He threw a handful of shrimp on the grill. Alive! He held them down with his flat silver spatula as they squirmed on the hot surface. He didn't even wince. I had heard that lobsters scream when you boil them. I wondered if shrimp scream too. If they did, I couldn't hear them over the sizzling sound.

I closed my eyes, but my dad nudged me under the table.

"Smile," he said.

I couldn't smile. The chef was murdering these poor little shrimp right in front of me.

Once the life was squashed out of them, the chef took his knife and sliced off the shrimp's feet in one fell swoop. Then he lifted the feet into the air and dropped them onto a small plate in front of me. They looked like toenail clippings.

"You have to be kidding me," I mumbled.

The businessmen stared at me with anticipation.

"Dad, I cannot eat this."

Under his breath, he spat, "You are to eat it. And you are to like it."

I grabbed the dead feet with my chopsticks and placed them in my mouth. I tried to chew, but couldn't. It was like putting an insect into my mouth. I swallowed as fast as I could.

Gulp.

The sharp ends dug into my throat, scratching their way down to my stomach. I gagged and coughed. My eyes got teary. I felt sick. I wanted Keiko to pick me up and take me back to the hotel.

The men waited for me to put my chopsticks down and then smiled and bowed repeatedly with delight.

For the rest of the meal, I remained shell-shocked and silent. I ate my beef and vegetables like a good girl.

As we were getting up to leave, I looked at my father and said, "I want to go back to the hotel."

"The night is not over," he said, pushing me forward.

Twenty minutes later, we were sitting in a dark, basement piano bar. The men were staring at me again. What did they want from me? Why were they smiling? Why was my dad doing this to me?

"Pick a song," my father said, directing me with his head toward the piano.

"Dad, I don't sing."

"Get up there and sing," my father said, again under his breath.

I walked over to the piano and asked to see the song sheets. I flipped through them and found a song I knew. My mother was the singer. She had sung some sexy French song at my Bat Mitzvah. She should be the one singing in front of these men. She should be the one saving my father's business. I stood up straight, my feet as close together as possible, arms folded across my chest, right next to the piano.

The men were lined up on a leather bench flush against the wall, waiting for me to open my mouth.

"Some say love it is a riveeeeer that drooooowns the tender reeeeeed," I sang.

They smiled and stared. One of them was staring at my breasts.

I continued to sing, "With the suuuuun's love in the spring beeeecooooomes the rooooooose."

Two months later, my father had to sell the company.

★   ★   ★

"I don't think it's a choice," I say to Iris. "I've always been stuck on the wheel, getting banged up, knocked around. Isn't that just the way it is?" I ask.

"It doesn't have to be," she says.

"I feel like my life has been in constant flux from the day I was born. We moved around a lot, always adjusting and readjusting to new environments. We didn't have much money in the beginning, then we were on top of the world, then we lost everything, then in our darkest moment, a miracle happened. My brother's tumors were finally re-moved—"

"Brother? Tumors?"

Oh, yeah, I haven't told you yet.

"I have a younger brother named Michael. We call him Mikey. Anyway, when he turned two, we were living in Tulsa, Oklahoma, and the doctors there discovered some kind of mass growing in his left cheek and thought it might be cancer. Obviously, my parents freaked out. They found the best ear, nose and throat doctor in the country, Dr. Hugh Biller, who practiced at Mount Sinai in New York City. Dr. Biller opened Mikey up and found tiny, benign tumors lining the facial nerve in his parotid gland, which is here," I say, rubbing my cheek. "Anyway, they couldn't remove all of them without risking paralysis, so they took out what they could. It was excruciatingly painful for my brother. He couldn't play sports. Kids teased him. From the age of two to twelve, he had five surgeries, and finally, when he was twelve, Dr. Biller was able to extract the rest of the mass without causing permanent paralysis to the left side of his face," I say, and inhale.

"Is that another one of your spiels?" Iris asks.

Whoa. No one has ever called me on that before.

"Yeah, I guess it is," I stutter. "It's hard for me to talk about my brother. I only brought him up to say that I understand that thing in life. When you're on top, there's nowhere to go but down. When you think you're down for the count, there's nowhere to go but up. Oh, duh. 'Round and round and round in the circle game,'" I talk-sing, finally getting the punch line.

"We can't control what happens in life, Kimberlee, but we can control how we react to it. We don't have to let it knock us around so wildly."

"Oddly enough, my father rides the cycles of life like a master. He just forges ahead, never letting the ups or downs get to him or change the way he feels about himself. He's amazing that way."

"I believe the reason you pulled the Fool as your indicator card and the Wheel of Fortune in your past environment position is that you have felt very out of control in your life. Powerless and small. And you're feeling that way again now. Am I right?"

I nod.

"And you look around and think other people seem to have more control over their lives—"

"And they do. Everyone I know seems to navigate their lives with such ease."

"It's important to feel your life from the inside out, as opposed to what most people do, which is to define their worth from the outside in. It gets you in trouble every time."

"I just feel like I try so hard."

"Yes, you try to control everything, but can't seem to control anything. It's really quite funny, Kimberlee. You're obsessed with knowing the future, thinking it will give you comfort, and yet, you do not believe in the future. You don't trust the cycles of life, or trust yourself to know how to ride them."

THE LOVERS.

Los Enamorados / Les Amoureux
Arcana: VI
Path on Kabbalah Tree of Life: 17
Color: Orange
Planet: Gemini
Constellation: Eagle, Antinoüs, and Sagittarius
Musical note: D

chapter three
the lovers

"The only journey is the one within."
—RAINER MARIA RILKE

*O*kay, *so I'm a control freak who doesn't trust
the future. So what? I'm not a murderer. I'm not a pedophile. I'm
just scared of fucking up again.*

"Your real problem," Iris says, picking up the next
card, "is the Lovers."

Tell me something I don't know.

I snap the card out of her hand to look at my "real
problem" closer up.

Adam and Eve in the Garden of Eden?

Eve stands in front of an apple tree, unabashed, and

unaware that Adam is buck-naked three feet to her left. Adam is aware of Eve, but doesn't seem all that interested in her. Both are sans pubic hair, making them look more like oversized children than lovers. I squint at Adam. He actually reminds me of my ex-boyfriend Zach. Aside from his lack of pubic hair and desire, both of which Zach had in spades, they look alike. They have the same body shape and the same light brown wavy hair.

Zach.

Zach and I broke up over ten years ago, but there will always be a part of my heart stuck on one of his mixed tapes along with Jim Morrison's "Indian Summer," Peter Gabriel's "Solsbury Hill" and Elvis Costello's "I Want You."

We met at New York University's Tisch School of the Arts in 1990.

I was living with my parents and younger brother on Central Park West and Eighty-eighth street. We had moved there at the end of my senior year, right before I graduated high school. I thought I might be upset about not living in the dorms, but when school started up in September, I was happy. I liked having my own bedroom. I liked that the fridge was always stocked. I liked being close to my mother. Even though I had just turned eighteen, I wasn't quite ready to be a woman.

Or was I?

Sometime in early October, my body started to speak on my behalf. It was 3 P.M. on a Tuesday. The sun was filtering in through the windows of the third-floor dance studio. The room was hot. Zach was wearing beat-up green polyester shorts, not the sexiest look, but I couldn't stop staring at his "package" as we walked in a big circle, listening to our teacher, Ron, a flamboyant gay man, command us to move our arms, "up and to the side, up and to the side."

I wondered if Zach noticed my body, if his insides were going haywire too. I was wearing a black leotard and purple tights and thought I looked good. But the other girls in the Circle in the Square acting program were stiff competition. Suzanne, being a former ice-skater, had the best body in class. Her ass simply didn't jiggle. Clair—an Elizabeth Taylor look-alike—refused to wear a bra. You could see her nipples through her tank top. And Heather, with her shiny black hair and nose ring, had a Goth-hot thing going on. Plus, I didn't like the way she looked at Zach.

"Stop and run in place," Ron screamed.

Zach and I stood directly across from each other, eyes locked. Everything about him was big: his body, his hands, his feet, his eyes. He wasn't a boy. He was a man. And looking at him made me feel like a woman. I wanted to scream out loud from across the circle, "You make me feel, you make me feel like a natural WOMAN."

Thank God, I didn't.

Later that week, our voice teacher Pat told us to choose partners for a warm-up exercise. Zach picked me. I felt my knees turn to jelly as he walked over and brushed up against me.

"The voice only has resonance if the body is completely relaxed," Pat explained. My body was most certainly *not* relaxed. "Before we begin vocal exercises, I want you to take turns massaging your partner," she instructed us.

The girls screamed in delight. One of the other guys in class whooped like Arsenio Hall. Zach smiled. I stood there shaking.

What kind of school was this anyway?

I lay down on the hard wooden floorboards and held my breath, thinking I'd feel less that way as if I were wading into ice-cold water.

Zach started with my feet.

A small sound escaped my lips. I turned it into a clearing-my-throat sound, embarrassed by my transparency. My face was red, my breathing heavy. He slowly made his way up my legs. He kneaded my calves, then my thighs. A woman had stomped on my back when I was in Japan, but this felt nothing like that. This was torture of a different kind. I thought I might cry or faint or throw up.

When it came my turn to do him, I pushed my fingertips into his naked feet and felt powerful. I could see the pleasure spill across his face, the corners of his mouth melting back toward his ears. As I got closer to his "area," his pleasure grew, literally. I wasn't sure if it was me specifically turning him on, or if he would have gotten a boner with any girl. Then I panicked and looked around the room, afraid people might be staring at us. I was relieved to see that everyone else was too busy writhing in their own pleasure to notice ours.

I couldn't believe that I—kissed-twice Kimmi—was attending some orgy of a school with a bunch of loosey-goosey, touchy-feely, incestuous actors who seemed a little too comfortable with their bodies.

Zach and I thanked each other at the end of class, my face still red, and took subways in different directions home.

For the next several weeks, I woke up early to curl my hair. I wanted to look pretty for him. I wanted him to like me, but Zach was a hippie complete with Birkenstocks and socks. Hippies never liked me. I was too fancy for them in my cashmere sweaters and silk scarves. Still, I sectioned my hair into pieces and rolled each strand with a huge hot curler. As I waited for the heat to do its magic, I applied my new Victoria Principal makeup. Then I took out the rollers, bent over, ran my fingers through my hair, flipped back up and voilà! I was one of Charlie's Angels. I sprayed Opium behind my ears and walked to the C train, my curls bouncing up and down with each step. I smelled like cinnamon, ylang-ylang and vanilla. Zach smelled like unwashed skin. I liked that smell. I liked that he was everything I wasn't.

It took one month of curling and bouncing and smiling and massaging for Zach to ask me out. It was the end of October. The air was cool. The leaves were falling. And the plan was to meet in front of Bobst Library on Washington Square Park and research Bertolt Brecht for our Experimental Theater class. So what if it was just a "study date." I didn't need dinner; I needed to be near him.

As I approached the building, I could see Zach standing

in front, his six-foot-two frame looming over everyone, his brown hair blowing around like leaves. I felt a shiver when our eyes met. I smiled. He nodded. He was too cool to show me a toothy grin.

We spent hours wandering through racks of books together, revealing the details of our lives, the names of siblings, cities we had visited, music we liked. At one point, his arm grazed my breast and I felt my entire body burn. Every inch of me was on fire. I tried to act casual, but my face flushed, and I'm pretty sure my pupils dilated. I giggled awkwardly and pointed to a copy of William Blake's *The Marriage of Heaven and Hell* for no apparent reason.

"I've never read Blake," I said, twirling my hair, cocking my head to the right.

He whipped out his wallet. "Wanna see something?" His voice was so deep, I thought I might fall in. I was expecting him to show me a Blake poem. Instead, he pulled out a photo. "This is Maggie, the girl who broke my heart," he said.

I grabbed the picture from him. Who was this Maggie girl? Was she pretty? Prettier than me? Her eyes were blue-green. My mother used to tell me that blue eyes were prettier than brown and that blue-eyed blondes were the prettiest women on earth. My eyes looked like dark brown M&M's and my hair was the color of night. Maggie's hair was strawberry blond, more orange than blond. I wondered where that fell on the pretty scale. I stared at Maggie's wallet-sized class photo for what felt like an hour. I wasn't sure why, but she made me want Zach more. I wanted to win him from her.

A week later, Zach invited me to see *Henry & June*. We sat in the fourth row, right of center. The lights dimmed. The previews played. Then the movie started. I could see his profile in the flickering light and wondered what he was thinking. I uncrossed my legs and fidgeted in my seat, looking back and forth between him and the screen. He kept his eyes straight ahead the entire time, his head perfectly still. I was starting to think he had forgotten about me, but then he pressed his leg against mine and grabbed my thigh. I could feel the heat from his body enter me, seep through my clothes and sink into my skin. I bit my lip and reached over for his leg, our arms now crisscrossed. My thighs quivered as we rubbed each other's legs, watching Fred Ward and Uma Thurman and Maria de Medeiros (who would later play Bruce Willis's girlfriend in *Pulp Fiction*) kiss and grope and fuck on screen.

When the movie was over, Zach walked me home, his arm wrapped around my waist the entire time. There was something about his size and the strength with which he held me that made me feel protected, small even. It's hard to feel small at five-eight. When we got to my building, we stood facing each other. He bent down, held my face in his hands and kissed me good night. Our first kiss: warm, wet, deep.

We spent the next month kissing on corners underneath yellow-lit streetlamps, fooling around to Ella Fitzgerald and Miles Davis, watching Woody Allen movies, his head buried in my neck, his winter coat smelling like me, like Opium.

When he *finally* invited me to his dorm room—his roommates were out for the night—I saw that he had a framed picture of Maggie on his desk. As I approached it, I noticed a burgundy silk painting hanging on the wall with a poem scrawled across the fabric in gold cursive. "Love, Maggie" it said at the bottom.

I felt hot again. This time from jealousy.

I didn't paint on silk. I didn't write poetry. I was pretty, though. I knew he thought I was pretty. Maybe it was a sex thing? Zach and I had kissed and dry humped and felt each other up over our clothes, but he had never seen me naked and we still hadn't gone to third base. I turned around and asked, "Was Maggie a good lover?" desperate for "no" to be the answer.

Zach was sitting on his bed, flipping through a magazine. "We never had sex," he said, continuing to flip the pages, his head still down. "When I had sex with Jennifer, it ruined everything. Made things weird. I didn't want that to happen with Maggie. So no. We never had sex. But we broke up anyway." His eyes seemed to droop more than usual. I hated her hold on him. I hated her blue-green eyes and her strawberry blond hair and her stupid happy smile. I wanted to smack her.

I excused myself to the bathroom and came out moments later half naked, wearing a see-through turquoise matching bra and panty set my mother had given me. As I made my way over to the bed, I could feel the night air ripping through the room. The windows were single pane and loose. I tried to keep my arms at my sides so he could see my body, but I felt too exposed, too chilled. I crossed my arms over my chest and walked the rest of the way.

"You're. Gorgeous. Really. Gorgeous," he stammered.

Zach scooted over and lifted the covers for me. He seemed bigger than usual. I worried he might crush me. We kissed. Then he gently caressed me, up and down, back and forth, in circles, tiny circles, causing all the hairs on my body to stand on end. I warmed up right away and relaxed with every touch. I felt his breath in my ears. His lips on my neck. His hands on my breasts . . . on my tummy . . . I gasped. His fingers had found their way inside me. I was levitating. Higher and higher. When I came, I shook so hard, he had to hold me down. My breath eventually returned to normal as we lay side by side in his twin bed. The light from the street was casting shadows on the wall. It was quiet. Too quiet. And then Zach started to sing, "Almost bluuuue, almost doing things we uuuused to doooo."

"What's that?" I asked.

"Just a song," he said, and continued to sing. "There's a girl here and she's almost you."

"Why are you singing that now?" I asked, flipping over onto my side, staring at him, examining his face, waiting for an answer.

He didn't say anything.

"What are you thinking about, Zach?"

I propped myself up, all the blood in my body now stirring from worry.

"She haunts me," he said. "I can't get her out of my head."

I crawled off the bed and made my way to the bathroom in the dark. I felt around for the light switch and shut the door. Dropping onto the cold, dirty tile floor, I sobbed silently, holding my breath, not wanting him to hear me.

He was asleep when I got back. His face looked peaceful and sweet. I loved him. I couldn't help it. He was the first boy to see me naked. The first boy to give me an orgasm. He was my first everything so far. I wished I could be his first something. But all his firsts were taken.

I thought the more time we spent together, the less he would think about Maggie, but the more time we spent together, the more *I* thought about her. She went from haunting him to haunting me. Whenever I saw a redhead on the street, it didn't matter what kind of redhead—tall, short, young, old, fat, skinny, with freckles, without freckles, walking a dog, eating a hotdog—I followed her. I wanted to see what she had that I didn't. I thought if I had red hair, if I painted on silk, maybe he would love me too.

"I'm starting to feel about you the way I felt about Maggie," he said, almost six months after our first kiss, two weeks before summer break. "I think I'm falling in love with you, Kimberlee."

"Really?" I said, afraid he might change his mind. I ran over to him and jumped onto his lap, kissing his face, his neck, his shoulders and chest. "I love you too, Zach. I love you so much, it hurts."

the lovers

It was Saturday, May 4, 1991.

My parents were away for the weekend and my brother was staying with friends, so we had the apartment to ourselves. We took off all of our clothes and started the water running in my parent's dark green marble bathroom. It had a hot tub big enough for four people and an adjacent standing shower. We turned the jets on high and washed each other's bodies, the soap slipping in and out of our hands, getting lost in the bubbles. When we were done with the tub, we hopped in the shower, rinsed off and then ran naked into my bedroom, leaving a trail of watery footprints on the mahogany parquet floor.

Zach threw me onto the bed and climbed on top of me, still wet, his hair dripping onto my face, neck and breasts. He placed his penis at the opening of my vagina and pushed gently. Nothing happened. He pushed again. Still nothing. He pushed one more time and it slipped in halfway.

Oh my God. Was this really happening? We had talked about having sex. I had just gone on the Pill. But now? Right now? Were we really going to do it?

I looked up at him and waited for him to say something. I wanted him to say, "I love you, Kimberlee, more than I've ever loved anyone, more than Maggie, more than life itself. I want to be inside you forever." Instead, he said, "Please, Kimberlee. Please. It's been such a long time since I've been inside a woman."

And just like that, I was no longer a virgin.

He went in the rest of the way, and then out, and then in, and out.

We were doing it. *I* was doing it.

Zach thrust some more and closed his eyes.

"Look at me," I said, tapping him on the back. My wet hair felt cold against my skin.

He opened his eyes, but then closed them a second later.

"Look at me. Please look at me!" I pleaded.

He opened his eyes wide this time, the way a person does when they're driving late at night and don't want to fall asleep. Even though he said he loved me, I wondered if he was still thinking about Maggie, imagining her beneath him instead of me.

"I think we should stop," I said.

"I thought you were on the Pill," he grunted.

"Yeah, but I'm only on day six. The pamphlet said I should wait seven days before having unprotected sex. I didn't know we'd be doing this tonight. I think we should be careful."

"Fine," he said, pulling out, standing in front of me, naked, hard and annoyed. "Does your brother have any condoms?"

"I hope not," I said.

"I'll check." He ran out of the room and came back a couple minutes later with a blue Trojan in his hand. He slipped it on and put himself back inside me. The condom felt weird, though, so we stopped and fell asleep.

Zach left the next morning, kissing me good-bye on the forehead.

I was expecting him to send me flowers, leave a voice mail message, something to acknowledge what had happened. When I hadn't heard from him by Monday night, I called.

We met up at a coffee shop near Washington Square Park and he explained that he didn't want to give "the sex thing" too much power. He didn't want things to get weird between us. But things *were* weird. He was being a dick and I was upset. He didn't apologize. But he did kiss me. That's all it took. That's all it ever took with him.

We had sex a few more times before he left for the summer. He tried to be better about keeping his eyes open, and I tried not to talk as much.

When Zach flew home, I wanted to go with him. I was dreading having to spend the summer by myself in Katonah, New York, where my parents were moving because they could no longer afford the city, or Dalton, the private school where my brother and Dustin Hoffman's kids went. Zach, on the other hand, had lots of friends, a whole life waiting for him back in Denver. I envied his long-standing history with a place. I wished I had friends from kindergarten and that my parents would stop moving.

I got a job at the local deli in Bedford Hills, where I made turkey sandwiches for hungry passersby—a far cry from modeling in Cologne and Paris. And at night, I listened to "Riders on the Storm" while staring at Zach's red

Lava lamp dance in globs or rereading his love letters. He sent me a new one every week, expressing his love for me, how much he missed me, how he couldn't wait to see me again. He told me about his friends, his cats, his dog, the lemon cake his mother had made him. We couldn't afford to speak on the phone, but one night he called me and seduced me into phone sex. Another first for me.

I spent the summer counting down the days until we'd be together again. I was going to visit him in Denver for my birthday in August.

From the second I landed to the moment I left, Zach and I couldn't keep our hands off each other. We drove from the airport to a Motel 6 to have sex. We had sex in the back of his Honda. He went down on me in a rowboat on a lake near his parents' house. At night, we made out under the stars for hours and slept intertwined in his twin bed. From the outside, everything looked normal; we looked like lovers in love. But something in me ached. Even though he had stopped talking about Maggie, I felt her presence with us, following us. When he showed me his high school, I wondered if they had kissed on the bleachers by the football field. When he took me to the local movie theater to see *Doc Hollywood*, I imagined him feeling her up in the dark. I tried to get her out of my head, but she had become part of me, part of my craziness. Thinking about her made me feel unlovable or maybe I felt unlovable already and used her as an excuse.

When school started up again in the fall, my craziness morphed into full-blown depression. My parents had rented me a studio apartment on Waverly Place instead of putting me in the dorms. I thought I'd like the freedom and independence, but I hated that no one knew if I came home at night. No one knew if I ate, if I brushed my teeth. I spent most of my nights crying for hours. Sobbing for no real reason.

Zach bought me two goldfish, Muffy and Fido. He wanted me to have company on the nights he wasn't there. It was sweet, but watching two orange fish swim around in their poop all day didn't make me feel better. Zach—wanting to be a normal college kid who drank beer and smoked weed—was tired of taking care of me. After witnessing my slow but steady spiral downward, he told me, "Being with you is kind of like being with my sick dog, Barkley. I love him, but it makes me sad to see what he's become." When Zach looked at me, I could tell he no longer thought of me as the fancy girl from the Upper West Side with curled hair. I thought back to Maggie's picture and her smile and loathed myself for not being happier.

On November 25—Maggie's birthday—sixteen days after our one-year anniversary, just before Zach left for winter break, we broke up over chamomile tea. I was tired of thinking about her. I was tired of feeling so sad all the time.

It was over . . . for three weeks.

★ ★ ★

"I don't know why," I say to Iris, "but this card reminds me of something my college boyfriend, Zach, broke in me. Something bigger than my heart."

"What could be bigger than your heart?" Iris asks me, seeming offended, as if I just took the Lord's name in vain.

"My purity?" I respond, unsure, never having voiced this feeling out loud.

"Come on, a bar of soap is pure. Babies are pure. What do you mean by purity?"

"It's something you can't get back once it's gone," I say.

"What exactly was taken from you?"

"My virginity, but that's not what I'm talking about. I used to be open, like the woman in this card," I say, and point. "I loved purely."

"Zach took that away?"

"No, but the relationship really fucked—sorry—the relationship really *messed* with my head. You know how when a person is allergic to yeast, they crave yeast. I read that in a magazine a few years ago. Well, Zach was kind of like that for me. I craved him even though he was bad for me. He was still in love with his ex-girlfriend when we were together and I kind of spiraled from there."

"It's interesting that you picked up on the love-triangle aspect of this card. In other versions, from other decks, there is often a man and *two* women depicted. The man is shown standing in between his 'wife' and his 'lover.' He doesn't know which woman to choose, the virgin or the whore."

"Are you saying I was the virgin and his ex-girlfriend was the whore?"

"No, Kimberlee. It's about integration, the need to

become whole. The 'virgin' and the 'whore' are actually aspects of the *man*. Until he learns to integrate them, he will always feel torn in two directions."

"I felt whole when I was with Zach."

"That's a sure-tell sign you weren't," Iris says with a chuckle. "Whenever we look to someone else to make us whole, we're not doing the work."

"I was definitely codependent."

"I hate that expression," Iris says. "Such psychobabble."

Oh, and "integrate" isn't?

"The Lovers card is about unifying opposite aspects. Light-Dark. Good-Evil. Love-Hate. We often choose partners who bring out our shadow selves. Romantic love is rarely about the other person."

"But I loved him."

"He reflected something beautiful in you. Lovers do that. They show us our beauty and our pain."

"He definetly showed me both," I say, staring down at the red mountain peak separating Adam and Eve.

"When we bury our pain, the deeper it goes, the darker it grows, the less access we have to it, and then someone comes along and rips open our preexisting wounds. That's how it works."

"Well, that makes me feel better."

"Sarcasm does not suit you," Iris says, and takes the card from me, placing it back in the spread. "The Lovers card could be anywhere in this spread. It happens to be showing up as your obstacle position, which makes me wonder in what ways *you're* still split."

★   ★   ★

Over winter break, two thousand miles apart, Zach and I got back together.

"I have something to tell you, baby. It's really hard for me to say, but I was at this party the other night, and well, we were all just chillin' out, and I dunno, somehow, well, somehow, I ended up on the couch, and there was this girl, she wasn't very pretty, but she came over to me and well . . ."

This can't be happening. We just had phone sex. He told me he loved me.

"And well, she unzipped my pants and started to give me a blow job. I know, baby. I'm so sorry. I got really grossed out and stopped it. Baby, I swear. I stopped it and then went home to take a shower. I'm so sorry. I had to tell you. I get back to the city in a few days. Baby, I'm sorry. I love you. I want to be with yo—"

The rest of his message cut off.

I walked over to my pink and yellow flowered couch, still in shock, and sat down. I pulled up my sleeve and started to pick my arm, looking for anything, a bump, a piece of dead skin, a mole. I picked until I bled.

My mother was the first person to pick my skin. I was nine years old. She held my arm in her hands and said, "You have bumpy skin like your father's." I had seen her pick my father's back by the swimming pool. She ran her fingertips over my skin and found a bump. She took her pointer finger and thumb and squeezed it until white stuff came out. I was mortified. I didn't want white stuff. I wanted it out. I wanted it all out. I started picking my skin after that. Whenever I was upset, panicked, sad, overwhelmed—whenever I felt anything at all—I picked.

I fell asleep a few hours after the phone message and didn't wake up the next day or the next or the day after that. It must have been day four when I heard knocking on my door.

At first, I thought it was a dream, but the knocking got louder, and I heard someone call my name.

I got out of bed, barely able to walk, and looked through the peephole at Zach's nose. I opened the door, wearing white cotton long underwear still warm from the bed. His skin was glossy from tears. I had never seen him like this. He was the strong one, the big one, but standing there in his $50 beat-up brown leather coat, he looked small. I stared at him with no expression, no joy or sadness. I felt nothing. I let go of the brass door handle and dropped my arm like a piece of spaghetti, walking back into my bright yellow apartment.

Zach followed me inside, took off his coat and reached over to hug me. I didn't resist or fight or pull away. We made love that night. He said he was sorry again and then kissed my arms.

A week later, I found myself calling information in Colorado Springs, where Maggie went to school. I had a gut feeling that she was the girl on the couch. Only he didn't stop her. He wasn't grossed out. He had fucked her and liked it and wasn't telling me. "Can you try Clarke spelled with an 'e' at the end?"

"There are too many listings for Maggie Clarke. I'll need a street address."

I wanted to dive into the phone line and strangle the operator. "Thanks anyway," I said, then pressed down the receiver, waited for a dial tone and called Zach. "I can't do this anymore. I can't be with you."

"What are you talking about?" Zach asked.

"I know you slept with Maggie."

"Kimberlee . . ."

"I won't get mad. I promise. I won't get mad. Just tell me." I said.

I could hear him breathing on the other end.

"I won't get mad," I promised again.

"Yes, I slept with Maggie," he admitted in a whisper.

"You fucking bastard! I never want to see you again," I said, and slammed down the phone.

I started gathering everything Zach had ever given me: books, cards, mixed tapes. I wanted nothing left of him in my apartment.

Fifteen minutes later, he was pounding at my door.

"Kimberlee. Let me in. I have to talk to you. Please."

I opened the door and threw his love letters at him.

"I'm sorry. I'm sorry. I'm so sorry," he kept repeating.

"How would you feel if I let some other guy put his dick inside me?" I asked, not sounding like myself; I had never been that crass before. "Maybe that's what I'll do."

Zach dropped to his knees, put his face in his hands

and sobbed. "Please, Kimberlee. Please. I'm sorry." He was snot sobbing at this point. I didn't care. I wanted him to cry. I wanted to watch him cry. But more than anything, I wanted him to take it back. I wanted him to love me so much that he never would have slept with Maggie in the first place.

After an hour of torturing him with mental images of me having sex with other men, I kicked him out and crawled back into bed.

I didn't get out for over a week.

I stopped showering. I stopped eating. I slept twelve to fifteen hours a day, and when I wasn't sleeping, I'd grab handfuls of Triscuits and listen to Sinéad O'Connor's "Nothing Compares 2 U" on repeat. Then Muffy, the girl goldfish, died and I thought it was a sign. I couldn't imagine jumping out my tenth-floor window, but I had fantasies of being hit by a city bus, having it knock me to the ground and crush me.

I didn't have a therapist, so there was no emergency number to dial. My mother was too consumed by her empty-nest depression to help me with my first real heartbreak, which was spiraling fast into something bigger. My brother and I didn't really speak. He was in high school, enjoying being a normal, good-looking kid for the first time in his life. I couldn't cry to my father. "Why are you being so female?" he would ask, as if being female and emotional were the same thing, and bad. He was sweet though. When he found out Muffy died, he got me four new fish so that I'd have a family.

When I didn't show up for class on the first day of spring semester, Zach left me a message. When I didn't show up the next day, he left me flowers at the front desk of my building. He wrote me a poem. He dropped off a chocolate croissant, my favorite. He left message after message on my answering machine. With each gesture of love, I came back to life a little more. I got out of bed. I ate some soup. I showered, and I eventually went to class, explaining to my teachers what had happened.

On Valentine's Day, I agreed to meet Zach for dinner. Something about his persistence made me think he really did love me. I put on my pink cotton sweater with the knit green frog on the shoulder and a black skirt that matched the button eyes of the frog. Looking in the mirror at my rosy cheeks and long brown hair with bangs, I caught a glimpse of the girl I used to be and smiled.

When I saw Zach's face, it felt like going home. He was as familiar to me as my childhood blanket. He kissed me gently on the cheek and escorted me into the restaurant, his hand resting on the small of my back. He seemed big again.

We smiled awkwardly and ordered Pasta Bolognese.

"Happy Valentine's Day, Kimberlee. I love you, I really do," he said, handing me a cutout paper heart with "KimKimKimKimKimKim . . ." written all over in red marker with the words "I love you" in blue marker placed in between the "Kim"s. Inside, he had copied a quote from *Zen and the Art of Motorcycle Maintenance*: "We've won it. It's going to get better now. You can tell these sort of things."

We got back together, but things didn't get better. It was different between us. Darker.

A few months later, in late April, we were in a Meisner Theater Company production of *The Lady's Not for Burning*, along with almost everyone else from our studio group, including nose-ring Heather—the girl I had suspected of having a crush on Zach.

On opening night, we were all warming up on the floor of the black box theater in The Shooting Gallery when an older couple holding flowers walked into the theater. Heather hopped up off the floor when she saw them, dropping her tough-girl act for a second, screaming, "Mom! Dad!" She ran over to them and gave them both hugs. Zach followed suit, shaking her father's hand and kissing her mom on the cheek. He had met them the summer before, on his way back to school in a U-Haul. He had swung by Detroit to pick her up. He told me he wanted someone "to share the driving and expenses" but swore they wouldn't share a motel room, that he would "sleep in the truck." I walked over to Heather's family, standing in a semicircle, introduced myself and pulled Zach backstage.

"Remember that time you and Heather shared a motel room driving back to New York?" I asked, becoming *that* girl, trying to catch him in a lie.

"Yeah, and?"

"You what?!"

"What, what?" Zach asked, confused.

"You fucking shared a room with her?!"

"You can't be serious. Nothing happened," he said, keeping his voice low.

And just like that, I snapped.

My fist clenched.

My right arm pulled back.

I punched him in the jaw.

Hard.

In front of everyone.

Zach stood perfectly still, his eyes darting around my face. I wasn't sure if he was hurt or mad or embarrassed that half the cast had just seen me clock him. I didn't care what he was. I didn't feel bad. I wanted to do it again.

And I did.

I started to punch Zach every time I got mad. When I found a journal entry in which he talked about wanting to have sex with another girl, I punched him in the arm with all my might. When I found out the brother-sister scene he was rehearsing with one of the prettiest girls in studio was actually a kissing scene, I punched him in the chest. It was as if someone else had taken over my body. I couldn't believe this was what I had become: a jealous, suspicious, psycho-girlfriend who was either hysterically crying or throwing punches.

★　★　★

"I feel like the whole ex-girlfriend, cheating episode broke something inside me, if that's what you mean by 'split,'" I say to Iris.

"Cheating?"

"Well, no, it wasn't really cheating. We were officially 'broken up' when it happened. But the timing was wonky. We had gotten back together over the phone. He didn't tell me what had happened. Then he did. But he lied. Then I found out. Then we broke up again. Our relationship was tumultuous, to say the least. We were on and off for a good four years. When I finally broke up with him in 1994, three years after the cheating incident, I still really loved him. I just didn't think I'd ever be able to trust him."

"It's usually ourselves we can't trust," Iris says.

"I certainly didn't love myself. I think men can smell low self-esteem on women. I had coffee with Zach a year or so ago and we talked about our relationship and what went wrong and I apologized for being so crazy and he admitted—and I can't believe he did this—he admitted to playing women against women."

"That's quite an admission."

"He was kind of making light of it, but said something like he thinks all women respond to competition. It didn't seem malicious when he said it. Just honest. When we broke up for good, he did the same thing to another woman that he had done to me: *I* was the girl he couldn't get over, and she worked hard to get him to love her more."

"That's tricky. We all need to love and trust *ourselves* more, which actually brings us to our next card, the High Priestess. . . ."

THE HIGH PRIESTESS.

La Gran Sacerdotisa / La Papesse
Arcana: II
Path on Kabbalah Tree of Life: 13
Color: Blue
Planet: Moon
Constellation: Cassiopeia
Musical note: G Sharp

the high priestess

"One does not become enlightened by imagining figures of light, but by making the darkness conscious."

—CARL JUNG

"Wait. That's it? We're done with the Lovers?" I say to Iris.

"A steak is *done*. We are finished."

"But what if I'm not *finished* with the Lovers?"

"No one is ever finished with the Lovers," Iris says, and grins. "These cards can stir something very deep in us. They might not make sense until much later."

"Much later as in later tonight or next year?"

"Ride the question, Kimberlee, ride the question," Iris says, handing me a blue-cloaked lady with a crescent moon at her feet, a scroll in her lap, a cross on her chest and a giant pearl on her head.

"I would just like to understand the 'split' stuff a little bit more."

"The High Priestess is in your hopes and dreams position," Iris says, barreling ahead. "It is separate from the rest of the spread and represents what you want more than anything, regardless of your current circumstances. It is what you are striving for."

The woman in the card is sitting in between two columns, one black, one gray. She looks like a nun draped in water.

This is what I should be striving for?

"I don't mean to sound like a broken record, but I don't get it. I don't see how *this* can be my 'dream card.' I have no intention of living my life in an abbey and I don't dream of women dressed in blue. I mean, I once kissed a girl, but I was very drunk," I say, trying to make a joke.

"Look again," she instructs, not finding me cute.

I didn't realize this was read-your-own-tarot-cards night.

"Kimberlee, every person sees something different."

I zoom in on the High Priestess's feet; she seems to be an extension of an ocean behind her. I laugh, not one of my sharp, high-pitched, make-grown-men-jump laughs, but still loud enough to startle a baby. "I don't know why, but this reminds me of a drumming experience I had in

college," I say. "Clover, a hippie from Berkeley, California, told me I needed to get in touch with my animal
spirits."

I was twenty-one and considered myself rather new
agey. I had read Dan Millman's *Way of the Peaceful Warrior.* I
had placed rose quartz crystal next to my bed for love. I
ended my outgoing answering machine message with a
nod to Quantum Psychics: "Create a cool day," which,
looking back now, was downright goofy. But animal spirits? Please.

After scarfing down Domino's Pizza, Clover told me to
lie down on her dorm room floor and relax while she got
everything together. It was hard to relax, though. The
floor reverberated with each pounding step as she gathered
the various items needed for divining my animal spirit. I
didn't ask any questions. I stared at the walls and wondered
what color they were . . . *Pumpkin? Coral? Flesh?*

"Close your eyes," she said, and knelt down beside
me, smelling of patchouli and pepperoni. She was holding
a dream weaver, a drum, headphones and what looked like
a small bundle of hay wrapped in string. I closed my eyes
and, a few seconds later, heard her light a match.

"What's that?" I asked, my eyes still shut. "It smells like
pot."

"It's a smudge stick. Dried sage. Native Americans use
it to clear out energy. It's especially good for cleansing old
or bad energy."

I had once eaten sage in a chicken dish, but I had never

smelled it burning, and I had certainly never been "smudged" before.

After she finished covering my entire body with smoke, she placed the headphones on my ears and said, "Okay, I'm going to push play. Once you hear the drums, you must go to a tree in your mind, any tree, and dig a hole. The hole will be your access to the underworld. It looks a lot like this world—trees, grass, hills, mountains. Any animals you encounter two or more times are your animal spirits. Listen to what they have to say. Then, when you hear the drumming speed up, it means your session is coming to an end, and you must thank your animal spirits, offer them a gift and then open your eyes. Got it?"

"Got it," I said. I *so* did not get it. I was supposed to find a tree, dig a hole and slip into the UNDERWORLD?

Clover pushed play, and the drumming began.

BOOM.

BOOM.

BOOM.

The drums felt like rushing water in my ears, washing away my thoughts. I stared at the black shapes squiggling around behind my eyelids and tried to imagine I was sitting under a birch tree in Vermont. What was I supposed to do again? Dig a hole? Yeah. She told me to dig a hole and slip into the underworld. Right, like that was going to happen. I started digging. And digging. And digging some more.

BOOM.

BOOM.

BOOM.

And then it happened, just as Clover said it would. I slipped into . . . God. Where was I? I looked around. I was floating smack dab in the middle of the ocean off the shores of the Napali Coast in Kauai, Hawaii, where my family used to spend summers when I was a kid. This was weird. And scary. I didn't want to be in the ocean. I tried to imagine myself on land, but I couldn't control my thoughts anymore.

BOOM.

BOOM.

BOOM.

I kicked my legs, trying to stay afloat, and looked down. The water was endlessly deep. I had no idea what was beneath me. A big stingray could come along and sting me. A whale could swallow me whole. What was I doing in the middle of the ocean?! I tried to calm down. "You like dolphins," I said to myself. "This is going to be great." But when I turned around, instead of seeing Flipper, I saw Jaws plowing through the water toward me. What the hell? Did I have my period? I'd heard sharks were attracted to blood. "Go away," I shouted, but he picked up speed. Fuck! What was I supposed to do? Play dead? I remembered back to Shark Week on the Discovery Channel. If you encounter a shark, you're supposed to stay completely still. I tried not to kick my legs, but it's hard to tread water while motionless. The shark stopped a few feet away from me and hovered in place. It was a standoff. Me and a gigantic shark with dead eyes and I'm-going-to-kill-you teeth.

BOOM.

BOOM.

BOOM.

What did he want from me? He was bigger than me. He could swim faster. He had sharper teeth. What did I have? I had . . . love. I wasn't sure why that was the particular thought that came to me, but I swam toward him to give him a hug. I could barely get my arms around his middle. He snapped his head around. I hugged harder, resting my head against his skin, which in real life would have torn my flesh, because in real life, sharkskin is made out of thousands of teeth-shaped pieces that become imbedded in whatever they're rubbed against. But this wasn't real life. This was insanity. And I kept hugging until my body relaxed. When he felt this shift in me, he swam out of my arms, spun around and . . . went down on me.

Iris looks at me in utter disbelief, mouth agape.

"Yes, you heard me right. The shark gave me oral sex."

I didn't feel his teeth. I just felt my body melting with pleasure, sinking lower and lower into the dark water, until finally we reached the bottom of the sea where what looked like the Emerald City illuminated everything. I didn't know what was happening or why, but I found myself dancing naked in the glowing green water as several sharks circled me like a goddess.

BOOM.

BOOM.

BOOM.

I could hear Clover breathing next to me and wondered if she knew I was swimming naked with sharks. I was beginning to think she had spiked the sage with pot. Or crack.

BOOM.

BOOM.

BOOM.

The sharks escorted me to shore and left me on the beach. The sand felt soft and hot in between my toes as I walked toward a cave fifty feet from the water and stepped inside. The raggedy black coral floor dug into my feet like broken glass.

First the ocean? Now a cave?

"Helloooooo," I shouted into the cavernous abyss, my voice echoing back.

Hundreds of bats whipped past me, making whooshing sounds in my ears. I stood still—cold and wet—wishing I had a sweatshirt.

Sharks and bats? These were my animal spirits? Why not a red-bellied frog? A hyacinth macaw? A puppy?

BOOM.BOOM.BOOM.

BOOM.BOOM.BOOM.

BOOM.BOOM.BOOM.

The drumming sped up as Clover had warned. I thanked the bats and headed back to the ocean. Oh, shit. I had forgotten to give the bats a present. I retraced my steps and threw a handful of small black bugs into the air for them to eat. I wasn't even sure if bats ate bugs. Then I crawled into the water and gave the sharks some steak—again, not sure if sharks ate cows. I knew they ate humans, so why not?

When the drumming finally stopped, I took off the headphones and cracked my eyes open. Clover was holding her Native American book open, ready to analyze my animals. "Sharks and bats," I said in a daze.

"Whoa," Clover said, and flipped through the pages. "Bats, okay, here we go. Bats. This is pretty cool shit. They mean rebirth. Shamanistic death. They mean you have to go through the darkness to get to the light, shed skin, face fear. Pretty heavy," Clover said, still flipping. "That's weird. Sharks aren't in here."

"Has that ever happened before?" I asked.

"No, never."

"Great," I said, feeling like a freak for getting busy with a shark, which apparently is not even a legitimate animal spirit.

"Did you know that sharks can smell one drop of blood in an area of water the size of New Jersey and that bats can detect objects as fine as a human hair using high-frequency sounds?" Iris asks me.

"Uh, no, I didn't know that."

"It's amazing your subconscious picked two of the most highly sensory creatures on the planet. Their survival depends on trusting their sense of the world around them."

"I remember standing in the cave, alone and naked, desperate for the sun to shine through a hole in the ceiling. I hate the dark. I was almost mad at the bats for choosing the dark over light. Then I realized they were experiencing the cave differently. They could see in the dark. Or rather, 'hear' in the dark," I say, correcting myself.

"That's what you're striving for," Iris says.

"To hear in the dark?" I ask.

"To make the dark light. To bring all of your hidden feelings, the feelings you judge or push down, to the surface. When you do that, you make the unconscious conscious. The High Priestess is the gateway to integration. She shows you what's inside."

"What if I don't like what's inside?" I ask.

"Then it gains control over you," she says. "Something else about the sharks—"

"Please don't make fun of me. I know it's sick to have sex with a shark," I say.

"Did you know the Polynesians used to believe in deities called 'aumakua'?"

"No," I say, feeling twelve again, as if I'm being grilled on the continents.

"These deities were called upon for protection, comfort and spiritual support. Some people still believe in making offerings to their 'aumakua.' Sharks may not be part of Native-American folklore, but they are most definitely considered 'aumakua.' Sharks protected Pele, the fire goddess."

"Well, I'm a Leo—a triple Leo, actually—so I have a lot of fire in me."

"And you made them an offering," Iris says.

"Yes, I did."

"I find it fascinating that you were initially afraid of the shark but that you overcame your fear through love. You trusted your instincts, even though they went against everything you *thought* you should do, what would be *normal* to do."

"Yeah," I say, not sure where she's going with this.

"That's what the High Priestess does. She takes the time to get quiet so she can listen to her inner voice. People often think their inner voice comes from their brain, but it doesn't. It's a purely instinctual thing. It uses all of your senses. We take in much more than we are aware of, so when we have a feeling about something, it is often smarter than our brain, it simply knows more. It takes a while to hear it and trust it."

Just then, out of nowhere, a black cat flies into the air, ninja-style, and lands on the back of Iris's chair. I jump back in my seat.

"No need to be alarmed. He's just a sweet old cat. Aren't you, Sage? Aren't you a sweet old cat?" she asks, pulling him into her lap.

"He just . . . I wasn't . . . You named your cat Sage?"

Iris strokes his body from head to tush, the blackness of his fur in stark contrast to the white of her skin. "Sage named himself," she explains. "He's an old soul. It's quite auspicious that he chose to show up for this card. The High Priestess represents trusting your inner voice, but it also happens to represent wisdom. In the Kabbalah Tree of Life, it's called Hochmah, which in Hebrew means 'unconscious thinking.' She is the bridge between conscious and unconscious."

"I don't feel so wise," I say.

"That's why she's in your dream position. You would like to be able to trust your inner voice and develop the wisdom to know the difference between instinctual and irrational fear."

★　★　★

"I clung to the canyon walls, crying my eyes out, screaming for my mother, as people rode by me on donkeys," I told a guy named Brad in our Performance and Art class at SUNY Purchase.

I had transferred there after two years at NYU. I didn't want to study acting anymore. I didn't want life to feel that dangerous, that raw. I was living at home with my parents again and commuting. Zach and I had broken up for the third time, so I spent most of my time alone, driving to and from school, doing homework and listening to Sarah McLachlan way too much. I felt lonely and lost, and to make matters worse, I got the worst haircut of my life *and* I went off the Pill, which caused my skin to break out in what the dermatologist called "a sea of blackheads and whiteheads." I looked like a pimple-faced LEGO man with a cap of plastic hair.

"I thought I was going to die. My leg muscles were burning. My skin was chafed. It took all the strength I had to hike the rest of the way up the Grand Canyon. One step. Two steps. Three. When I finally made it to the top,

I collapsed. If I had known I was going to have to hike fourteen miles in and fourteen miles out in a twenty-four-hour time period, I never would have signed up for the trip in the first place. I never would have subjected myself to such torture. But I pushed beyond my comfort zone and accomplished something I didn't think I had in me, and it made me realize how safe we all try to keep ourselves."

Brad stared at me expressionless.

"That's it. That's my story," I said, and sat back down. Even though I didn't know Brad, it felt good to tell him a story. It made me feel more connected and less alone. He listened to me, looked at me, acknowledged my existence. I needed that. "Okay, now you."

"Last semester," he began, tugging on his black soul patch, "I took this class called Shakespeare in Film. It was a boring class. But there was this girl. She wasn't the prettiest girl in the class. But she had really beautiful hair. She always sat up front. I spent the entire class looking at the back of her head. I like to draw, so I used to draw pictures of her hair." He paused. "In my notebook, you'll find hundreds of pictures of *your* hair."

My hair? Creepy. Not the prettiest girl in class? What was that supposed to mean? At least he liked my hair, or he did before I cut it off. I felt sick to my stomach and flattered at the same time.

After class, I heard his voice echo down the hall. "Hey, wanna get lunch?" he yelled, running to catch up with me.

"Uh," I said, lowering my head, so my hair would cover my face. "Sure."

We walked to the cafeteria through the courtyard, with no further mention of his notebook, talking about Anna Deavere Smith and Spalding Gray instead. Then we carried our orange trays to an outside table and ate turkey sandwiches in the sun. He told me he wanted to be a writer one day. I told him I had switched majors from Acting to Social Science in the Arts and had fallen in love with documentary film. For my senior thesis, I was making a documentary on "women and beauty." I wanted to break it up into four categories: physical beauty, emotional beauty, socioeconomic effects on beauty, and jealousy among women in friendships.

. . . women in friendships.

I wasn't sure what was happening. Were Brad and I becoming friends?

Our class met every Monday and Wednesday, and every day after class Brad would ask me to join him for lunch. On one particular Wednesday in late April, he asked me to join him for a study date in the library. Libraries made me think of Zach, but I went anyway.

As we made our way past the stacks to the back, Brad kissed me on the mouth hard and fast. It was almost as if he had never kissed a girl before.

We tried to study after that, but I couldn't concentrate.

Was *Zach* kissing someone else somewhere else? Or worse, was he sleeping with someone else? I wanted to be with Zach, not Brad. What was I doing?

After an hour or so, Brad walked me back to my car.

The sky was growing dark. We quickened our steps, but it started to pour before we reached the parking lot. We ran the rest of the way, trying not to slip on the pavement. I unlocked my car with the push of a button and we both jumped in, drenched. We were sitting in the front, out of breath, shaking the excess water off, when Brad looked at me with a seriousness that scared me. He reached over and pulled my wet bangs off my face.

"I like bangs," I said, pulling them back so they covered my forehead again. My mother had always told me I looked prettier with bangs. I had had them for as long as I'd had hair. We sat in silence and waited for the rain to stop. When it didn't let up, he said, "Screw it. I'll see you later." He opened the car door and ran across the parking lot to his dorm.

Later that week, I found a note in my sociology text-book. In sloppy handwriting, Brad had written:

It's interesting you said, "I like bangs." You didn't tell me to stop. You didn't say, "No, don't do that." You simply said, "I like bangs." People bothered with you, didn't they? They cared what you did. What you looked like. People never bothered with me. —Brad

I chose not to respond. He didn't bring it up. We carried on as if the bang incident had never happened.

"Hey, wanna have dinner at my place? My roommates are going out for the night. It'd be the two of us," he said the following week. No one had ever made me dinner before—

certainly not Zach, whose idea of cooking was Ramen noodles in the microwave—so I accepted the invitation.

I walked into Brad's apartment wearing a floral skirt and Birkenstocks, carrying a bottle of wine. He kissed me and told me to wait on his futon while he finished up.

"I made a glazed ham," he screamed from the kitchen.

I had eaten plenty of bacon in my life, but never a glazed ham. I thought ham was something you were supposed to eat on Christmas. Didn't he know I was Jewish?

"Sounds great," I said.

"It'll be ready soon," he said, and then excused himself to the bathroom.

I sat on the futon, staring at my reflection in the TV set. Ten minutes passed and he was still in the bathroom. I got up to check on him. I could hear him farting from the hallway.

"You okay in there?" I asked.

"I'm fine," he strained to say.

Squirt. Plop. Squirt. Fart.

I sat back down, still able to hear him. I was worried I might puke on his futon. I wanted to go home, but how could I leave? We hadn't even eaten dinner yet, so I continued to listen, my nausea growing by the second.

"Sorry about that," he said, and went into the kitchen to get the ham.

"This looks beautiful," I said, hoping he had washed his hands, the pink ham staring up at me from my plate. I took a bite. "I would eat it in a boat. I would eat it with a goat," I said, trying to lighten the mood.

"You don't like it?" he asked, as if I had just made a your-mama joke.

"No, it's great. I love ham."

After dinner, we moved to the futon, where I had listened to him poop out half of New Jersey. He leaned over and kissed me, putting his hand on my thigh.

"Brad, I'm not ready for that," I said.

"Come on," he said, leaning in closer.

"Seriously, Brad," I said, and pushed him off.

"It'll feel good," he said, and put his hand back on my thigh.

"Uh, no, I don't think so," I said, shoving him off for good. "I gotta go."

I grabbed my purse and ran out of his apartment. I kept running, all the way to my car, past a girl reading under a tree, past a group of kids singing "Stairway to Heaven" on a picnic blanket. I was covered in sweat by the time I got to my car. I locked the doors and raced out of the parking lot.

Brad wrote me an apology letter, but it didn't matter. It was over. The ham. The diarrhea. The groping. I was done. I didn't need to make it official. We weren't going out. We didn't need to break up.

School was almost over. I finished up my last days of classes, skipping the one we had together, and left without saying good-bye. I graduated and never set foot on campus again.

I thought I would never see or hear from Brad again, but two weeks into summer, I got an Elvis postcard:

Hi Kimberlee, I've been thinking of you. I hope you're feeling safe and that your hair is growing long. Love, Brad

I wasn't sure how he got my address or what he meant by "feeling safe." I felt plenty safe. I didn't respond and figured he'd get the hint. He didn't. Three weeks later, I got a letter:

Hi Kimberlee. I'm wondering why I haven't heard from you. (A) You've moved on. (B) You're desperately in love with me and scared. (C) You've joined a nunnery. I'm hoping it's B or C. And I hope you feel safe. Love, Brad

What was with this safe shit?

A few days after that, a 9 × 17 poster arrived in a tube. It was a pencil drawing of an oak tree and my face enlarged in the sky. I looked like an enormous cloud, tree branches overlapping my chin. On one of the branches, Brad had drawn himself, sitting in a Robin Hood outfit, looking up at my face. At the bottom, he wrote: "Two souls in the tree of life, Orpheus contemplates."

I sure as hell didn't feel safe anymore.

I ran downstairs to show my mother.

"Honey, maybe you should tell him to stop writing you," she said.

I ran back upstairs and ripped the poster to shreds.

Another package came the next week. This time, an audiotape. I put it in my tape deck and listened. "I miss you, Kimberlee. I think about you every second of every day." Then I heard rustling. "Please don't jerk off, please don't jerk off," I said aloud. "I'm going to sing you a song," he said. "It will probably be off-key, but you strike me as the kind of person who likes people for their messiness." Then he belted out "With or Without You," by U2. "On a bed of nails she makes me wait."

"This guy is going to fucking kill me!" I screamed.

I took it out and shoved it in a drawer. *Ignore him,* I kept telling myself. It had been two months since I had graduated. I figured he would give up soon enough.

I was wrong.

On August 10, the day after my birthday, my mother picked me up at the train station. I had spent the night with a friend in the city. As I approached the car, I could see through the window that my mother had a strange look on her face.

"What's up, Mom?" I asked, putting on my seat belt.

"That boy who keeps writing you letters, well, he showed up at the house yesterday with a manuscript. Kimmi, he wrote a book about you and America, saying the two things seemed like a natural fit. He wants to give it to you in person. I told him you were out of town and that you would call him when you got back in."

"A book?!"

"Kimmi, you have to call him and put a stop to this."

"Were you scared of him, Mom? Should I be scared of him?"

She took a second to answer. "I don't know. He just seemed sad to me."

When I got home, I shut my bedroom door and dialed his number.

He picked up on the first ring.

"Hi Brad, it's Kimberlee. Listen, I need you to know that I never loved you. I will never love you. And I never want to hear from you again. If you try to contact me, I will call the police. I was trying to be nice. I was trying to protect your feelings, thinking my silence would let you know I wasn't interested. But it didn't work and I need you to stop. Really. Please stop."

He was silent.

"Did you hear what I just said?"

"I thought you'd like being pursued, that I wasn't willing to give you up."

I didn't say anything.

"Kimberlee?"

"Yes?"

"If I ever run into you on the street, will you be nice to me?"

"Yes, I will be nice to you," I said. "But I have to go now. Good-bye."

I hung up the phone and felt safe for the first time all summer.

A month later, I moved into an apartment on West Thirteenth Street and Sixth Avenue with two women I knew from NYU. I was thrilled to have roommates. I painted my bedroom pink. I got a job as a page at CBS, and I worked at a coffee shop on the weekends.

Then I got a call from my brother. Whenever Michael

called, I got nervous. I always thought something was wrong.

"Kimmi, you're never going to believe this," he said.

"Are you okay?" I asked, holding my breath.

"Yeah. Yeah. Remember that guy you used to date? You know, the stalker dude? Turns out, he did the same exact thing to my friend Carla's friend who also went to Purchase."

"Are you serious?" I said.

"I don't know if she got a Robin Hood poster, but yeah."

I sat on the edge of my bed, unable to speak, imagining that Carla's friend had probably ignored red flags and pretended to like ham too.

III

THE EMPRESS.

La Emperatriz / L'impératrice
Arcana: III
Path on Kabbalah Tree of Life: 14
Color: Green
Planet: Venus
Constellation: The Virgin
Musical note: F Sharp

the empress

"Mothers be good to your daughters."
—JOHN MAYER

The first thing I notice about the Empress is how relaxed and confident she seems. The second thing I notice is her flowing, white dress with red roses on it. My mother used to wear similar muumuus when I was a kid. All different fabrics and colors. Cotton. Velour. Royal blue. Hot pink. They were big in the seventies—house robes, muumuus, whatever you want to call them—and my cuddly-as-a-bear mother knew how to rock them out like a diva. If she had been born into royalty, she also would have worn a tiara like the one on top of the Empress's head.

"This card reminds me of my mom," I say to Iris.

"Very good. You're letting the cards speak to you," Iris says, nodding her head in approval. "The Empress represents the archetypal mother."

"She happens to look exactly like my mother. If my mother were petite and brunette, I probably wouldn't have made the connection."

"I've had many people pick up on the mother aspect of this card and their mothers were African American, Asian . . ."

"Maybe because she's wearing something that looks like a maternity dress?"

"You picked up on the lovers triangle aspect of the Lovers card and you had no idea about the other versions in which two women are depicted. The card sparked a feeling. That's what this is all about," Iris says.

"Well, this woman definitely reminds me of my mother," I say, staring down at the cushy orange throne, the gray heart, the red cushion, the golden wheat field, the evergreens, the river. . . .

★   ★   ★

My mother was different after the divorce.

She had lost a lot of weight and was finally feeling good about herself. She wasn't skinny, but she could get into size 12 jeans and her butt looked cute. With her blond hair, baby-doll face, breathy voice and new svelte body, she looked a bit like Marilyn Monroe, and attracted the attention of men everywhere: doormen, handymen, businessmen, men in Fairway, men in Starbucks, old men, middle-aged men, even men my age. She sauntered and smiled and batted her eyelashes like a sex kitten. She was fifty going on twenty. I was twenty-four going on twenty-five, not used to my new sexy mother. I wanted my old mom back, my big, cuddly, muumuu-wearing Mom.

It would have been one thing if she had stayed in Westchester or moved to California, where she could have strutted her stuff out of my sight. But she moved into my building on the Upper West Side. There was no escaping her.

"Kimmi, I was in the corner deli yesterday, and a gorgeous man, and I mean gorgeous, about thirty-five, maybe thirty, came over to me and said, 'You are the woman of my dreams.' Then he started to serenade me in front of the pineapples."

"Mom, you can't smile at everyone you see. You have to be careful."

"Kimmi. I'm having fun. I'm a grown-up. I know how to take care of myself."

I didn't believe her. She had let my father bully her all through their marriage. And she never, not once, put up a fight or told him to fuck off. When he called her a "stupid bitch" after finding out she had lied to him about taking his shirts to the dry cleaners, she cowered in the corner and simply said, "I'm sorry, Mark. I'm sorry." When he rated her apple pie in front of guests, giving her a six out of ten, after she had spent all afternoon peeling and soaking apples, she just smiled. *I* was the one who stood up to him. I was the one who jumped on his back when he lunged at her for accidentally breaking the answering machine.

Bullshit, she could take of care herself.

Now that she was finally free of my father, I worried there would be someone else like him, someone else who would hurt or mistreat her. What was I supposed to do, though? Stand outside her door with a baseball bat and screen the men who came to visit? I didn't have the time, and frankly, I didn't want to be reminded that my mother, twice my age, was getting more play than me.

"How is it having your mom in the same building?" my friends would ask. "Aren't you scared she's going to stop by unannounced when you have someone over?" Wink. Wink.

The truth was, I hadn't had a boyfriend since Zach and I hadn't had a date in over six months. While my mother was flitting and flirting all over New York City, and my father was living in Philly with his new wife, and my brother was studying Spanish in Costa Rica for college credit, I was living in a studio apartment six floors below my mother, working as a temp at Worldwide Television News, eating boxes of Entenmann's cookies and masturbating for entertainment. It was no life.

"Let's visit Mikey," my mother said as we sat on her couch in her living room, waiting for our chicken in lemon sauce from Miss Elle's to be delivered. That was another thing about my mother: after the divorce, she stopped cooking.

"In Costa Rica?" I asked. "Isn't that expensive?"

"I have money," she said.

She was getting alimony from my father, but not enough to be extravagant.

"Mikey can get us a discount on a room at the place he's staying," she added.

Why not? What did I have going on that was so special that I couldn't visit my brother in Costa Rica for his birthday and Thanksgiving, which fell within a couple of days of each other, along with Maggie's birthday, which I tried not to think about.

I asked my boss for a week off, and before I knew it, I was sitting next to my mother on a plane to San Jose. I looked down at her Lee Press-On Nails. This was going to be either fun or a total nightmare.

Mikey was waiting for us at the airport. I hadn't seen him in a while. Six months, maybe. The last time I saw him was when we were helping my mother pack up the house and move to the city. I reached up to hug him. He was tall and strong and tan, but when I looked at him, I still saw the cute, button-nosed boy I never appreciated as a kid. He grabbed our bags and helped us into the minivan.

It took us a little over an hour to get to Costa Verde, the small hotel where we would be staying in Quepos, overlooking Manuel Antonio National Park. Everything about the country—the lush greenery, the iguanas, the monkeys—felt wild, untamed, like our mother in her big straw hat.

I smiled at my brother, who looked at my mother and asked, "Are you going wear that hat every day?"

"Give me a break."

The room my mother and I were sharing was bigger than both our New York City apartments combined. It had a kitchen with a floating island. There was a hammock in the room and floor-to-ceiling glassless screen windows. It was like being in a treetop screened-in porch overlooking the ocean. I was in heaven and, for a second, forgot about my mother's men, my lack of men and my $10-an-hour job.

In the morning, we ate scrambled eggs with *pico de gallo* at the hotel restaurant while we watched monkeys swing from branch to branch. In the afternoon, we went to Café Milagro, where we played chess, drank coffee and listened to salsa music. Now *this* was living.

On our fourth night, a bunch of Michael's friends invited us to a popular outdoor nightclub right on the water. The moon was high in the sky, and I was wearing a red floral, sleeveless dress, cut on the bias, that hugged my body in all the right places. My mother was wearing a plain black dress fit more for a Westchester cocktail party than a night out in the jungle. I felt like shaking my tits in her face and saying, "Take that."

We sat down at a wooden table facing the dance floor, and the waiter came over and poured us shots of chilled red wine. I thought red wine had to be room temperature to be good, but this was delicious and refreshing, so we asked for more.

I didn't like to drink with my mother. She wasn't an alcoholic, but when she drank, she drank too much. When we were kids, she used to drink white wine at night and dance around to Sister Sledge. As we got older, though, as she got older, especially leading up to the divorce, wine had the opposite effect on her. It made her nasty and catty, and sometimes unrecognizable.

Michael was oblivious to our mother's alcohol intake as he flailed around on the dance floor with his friends. I decided not to worry about it either. Fuck it, we were on vacation. I wanted to dance too.

As I made my way through the crowd to the dance floor, a stranger grabbed my arm and handed me a sequined party mask. I put it on and started to dance, my hips swinging back and forth, my arms rolling up over my head and down again. I liked how my body moved. I liked the shapes it made and how my back arched when I flipped my head around. My mother shimmied up beside me, thrusting her hips into mine, trying to bump and grind with me. I wanted her off of me, away from me, so I spun around and danced to the outer edges of the dance floor. Dancing alone was better than dancing with her. I closed my eyes to get my rhythm back. When I opened them again, my mother was salsa dancing with a twenty-one-year-old local boy named Juan P.—"P" so they wouldn't confuse him with the other Juan.

I danced over to my brother, who was bobbing up and

down to the beat, head down, shoulders slumped. I lifted his chin with my finger so he could see our mother rubbed up against his friend.

"Mom's drunk," I said.

The look in his eyes was almost cartoonish. I thought I saw smoke coming out of his ears. He shoved past the other dancers who were shaking their rumps with abandon. The stranger who had handed me the mask tried to engage him in a crazy hand dance. My brother skillfully ducked down and around him. I trailed behind.

Our mother was in the middle of a forward thrust when Michael grabbed her arm hard, the way my father used to, and shouted in her ear, "Party's over. Time to go home."

On the cab ride back to the hotel, my brother kept asking, "How much wine did you have? I'm asking you a question. How much wine did you drink?" She refused to answer him and stared out the window.

"She's all yours," my brother said, dropping us off at our room.

"She's been mine for the last few months. You take her," I said.

"Fat chance," he said, and walked away.

"Mom, you wanna take a shower first?" I asked, kicking off my flip-flops. "Mom, I'm talking to you. Do you want to take a shower?" I asked again, stepping in front of her to make eye contact.

She said nothing.

"Fine, then. I'm getting in."

"Fine, then," she said, mocking my voice.

I took off my dress and underwear and placed them on top of the toilet seat, trying to forget about my drunken mother in the other room. I stepped in and stood still on the soft, smooth tiles, letting the cool water soothe me. I got out and wrapped myself in a towel. I was calmer, cleaner. I turned around to pick up my clothes and saw something moving. I bent down to look. Tiny ants were crawling all over the crotch of my underwear.

"EEEEWWWWW," I screamed.

My skin got all creepy-crawly. I swatted at the back of my neck only to find a lock of hair. Then something struck me. Silence. Why wasn't my mother coming in to see if I was okay?

Still dripping with water, I peeked my head out of the bathroom to see my mother's clothes lying in a pile on the floor.

Sweet Jesus.

I dropped my towel on the ground, threw on my night-gown and went to the porch to see if she was there. She wasn't. I looked down and saw her splashing around loudly in the pool. *Yikes!* I raced out of our room and knocked on my brother's door, across the hall. "Quick, Mom is swimming in the pool. I think she's naked."

"Are you kidding me?" he said, grabbing a shirt from the floor and putting it on.

I ran back into my room and watched from the balcony.

Splash. Splash. My mother had no idea what was coming.

Michael opened the gate to the pool and covered his eyes. In a firm, parental voice, he said, "Mom, get out of the pool RIGHT NOW. It's two A.M. You're going to wake up the other guests."

"No," she said, and swam to the other side.

"I said, NOW!" he screamed.

"FINE," she screamed back, and headed toward the ladder.

I went back inside and sat on the corner of my bed like a nervous mother awaiting the late arrival of her teenage daughter.

The door swung open.

She looked like a soaked puppy, thick, wet strands of hair covering her face. At least she was wearing a bathing suit.

"Are you okay?" I asked, reaching for her arm.

She was mumbling to herself.

"What? What are you saying?" I asked.

"Thanks a lot for siccing the gestapo on me," she said under her breath, shoulders hunched, head down, on her way to the bathroom.

The next morning, she got up before I did and went to breakfast without me. When I got to the restaurant, she was sitting across from my brother, who was reading the paper. Her hands were folded on her lap like a kid determined not to get into trouble anymore. I sat down. She poured herself some more coffee.

"So?" I asked her. "How are you feeling?"

"Fine," she said. There was no way in hell she was going to miss our rafting trip scheduled for later that morning.

"Are you sure you're feeling well enough to go?" my brother asked, looking up at her from the paper.

"I wouldn't miss it for the world," she said, getting up from the table, swinging her leopard-print sarong around her waist and tying it in a knot.

"Mom, I think you're going to need to wear shorts," he said.

"I don't wear shorts," she said, and walked off in a huff.

A couple hours later, my brother, his two local buddies, Carlos and Pablo, and a crazy Californian surfer dude named Scott, our rafting guide for the day, loaded the van with life vests and paddles and strapped the raft to the roof.

"You ready to rock the Naranjo?" Scott shouted, climbing behind the wheel.

"You betcha," my mother yelled out without hesitation.

"Not really," I said, staring at the green streak in his blond hair.

"The river is a pussycat," he said, and sped down the dirt road.

The bumpy back roads were starting to make me feel carsick. I looked out the window and tried to focus on the trees and the sky. It was a glorious day. Sunny. No clouds. Not too hot.

Scott finally pulled over and parked alongside a grassy road. My mother lifted some paddles onto her shoulder, her sunglasses concealing her hangover. I carried a string of life vests on each arm, and the boys hoisted the raft up and over their heads. Together, we schlepped the equipment through the rocky terrain for what seemed like half a mile. The river started to come into view. It was brown and opaque. Yuck. I didn't want to get into water I couldn't see through.

The boys, looking as rugged as the landscape in their ripped T-shirts and beat-up baseball caps, tossed the raft into the water and held it in place. My mother waded in after them. "Oooooh, it's sooooo cold," she cried. I fastened my Velcro sandals on tight before climbing over the slippery rocks.

The water was cold and rushing. It was hard to keep my balance. I handed everyone a vest. My mother handed me a paddle. Her long, blond hair was shimmering in the sun, her pink frosted lipstick looked out of place against the craggy riverbank.

We all held on to the raft as we listened to Scott give us the rundown:

"Okay, dudes, seriously. There are a few things you have to know, so listen up. One, if you fall out of the raft, never swim headfirst, make sure your feet are in front of you. Two, never try to stand up. Your feet could get caught in between two rocks and you could drown. I'm serious, dude. And I guess the other thing you gotta know is that you have to avoid the rocks. Paddle hard and follow my cue."

Hearing Scott call us "dudes" made me want to run

back to the van. Were we really going to get into a raft with this kid? Why wasn't my mother concerned? *Whatever.* I was tired of playing the heavy. What was the worst that could happen?

"You ready to rock out like a motherfucker?" Scott screamed as if he were about to dive into a mosh pit.

I turned to Carlos and Pablo to make sure they weren't looking at my mother, and then to my mother to make sure she wasn't looking at Carlos or Pablo.

Everyone piled in.

By the time I got my right leg over the lip of the raft, all the seats were taken except for the front position. Scott waited for me to get situated and then pushed off with his paddle. Just like that, we were headed down the river at a clip, trees and rocks and birds passing us by. The water was fairly calm. We barely had to paddle. Carlos and Pablo were speaking to each other in Spanish. Michael was telling my mother to be careful not to lose her sunglasses—she had already lost two pairs on the trip so far. I asked Scott, "Have you ever been on a trip and had someone fall out?"

"Not only do we lose a person each trip, but that person is almost always where you're sitting!"

Everyone burst into laughter. Except me.

Then the rapids picked up.

"Paddle, paddle, paddle," Scott screamed out. "Hard left," he yelled. "Hard right." Water was splashing in our faces. The paddles were heavy and slick. My foot kept slipping. With every bounce, I grew more certain that I was going over. My mother, on the other hand, couldn't stop screaming with delight. I could see her breasts bouncing up and down out of the corner of my eyes. I worried they might fall out of her bathing suit. And then BAM! The raft hit an enormous boulder and capsized.

Everyone fell out.

The rush of the rapids ripped off one of my sandals and pulled me under water. I couldn't see anything or anyone. I held my breath so I wouldn't swallow water, and reached my arms out for the raft. The surface was too wet and too smooth to hold. I found the rope and grabbed it with both hands and held on tight. I lifted my head and saw Scott running alongside the river. All at once, he jumped into the raft, like a stunt double from *Indiana Jones*, and managed to maneuver it over to shore, tugging me in along with it.

I got out and stood on the mud, my legs shaking violently. Carlos and Pablo were walking toward me from farther up the river.

I screamed out, "Where are my mother and brother?"

They said nothing.

"Where are they?" I screamed again.

"They're down the river," Scott said in a whisper.

I flipped around to look at him.

"I saw them go down," he said. He looked less like a badass rocker and more like a little boy who wanted his mommy. I wanted my mommy too.

Clouds were starting to form in what had been a perfect sky. The boulders now looked like enemy soldiers, scattered strategically in the water, intimidating us, daring us to get back in. I couldn't move. I couldn't breathe. I couldn't believe that I actually wished my father was there.

"Come on. Quick," Scott shouted to Carlos and Pablo. "We have to find them."

We were silent as we headed back down the river.

One hundred meters.

Two hundred meters.

Where were they? Why was it taking so long to find them? *Please God, please let them be okay. I'll be nicer. Really, I will be.* I was surprised to find myself praying. The only other times I had prayed to God were during my brother's surgeries. I remember being in the waiting area at Mount Sinai, silently saying, "Please God, make him be okay. I'm sorry I've been mean to him." I felt like it was my fault they were lost on the river, that my anger and jealousy had killed them.

Half a mile.

One mile.

"There they are! Over there!" Scott yelled, pointing to a muddy embankment.

My mother was flat on her back. My brother was squatting down beside her. Fifteen local kids were swarming around them like bees.

She wasn't moving.

"Faster," I screamed.

Scott paddled harder and steered us over.

I got out of the raft and ran. The kids moved back so I could get to her. Was she dead? *Please God, no.*

I heard her cough and started to cry. She was alive! *Thank you. Thank you. Thank you.*

I bent down and kissed her face, which was cold and clammy and smudged with makeup, black mascara running down her cheeks like Tammy Faye Bakker. She was spitting up water. Her skin was blotchy.

"Mommy, are you okay? Are you okay?" I asked.

"She's okay," my brother said, his hand planted on her shoulder.

"Are *you* okay?" I asked my brother.

"It was a rough ride," he said. "She was heading down the river headfirst, so I went in after her." Then he mouthed, "We almost lost her."

I kissed his hand and then kissed her face again.

"Kimmi, please, don't. I need to breathe," she sputtered. I backed away and stared at her. She just had a near-death experience—shouldn't she be clinging to me like a newborn?

"We have to get back in the raft," Scott said. "We have less than a mile to go before the van picks us up."

"No," my mother cried.

"Loryn, you have to," Scott said with surprising maturity. "You'll be okay. We have one more fall, but then we're home free. You've survived the worst of it."

The boys, who seemed more like men now, helped my mother up and walked her over to the raft. They lifted her legs one at a time and set her down in the middle.

Everyone took a seat on the edge of the raft, surrounding her on all sides. Scott pushed off slowly, heading us back down the river, swerving in and out of rapids without a hitch.

I kept an eye on my mother the entire time. She was a shivering mess. I had seen her cry before. I had seen her face turn red from too much wine. I had seen her look like a frightened animal with my father. But I had never seen her look like this.

When we got back to the hotel, my mother showered first. She was in there for a long time, so I knocked on the door. "Hey, Mom, you okay in there?" I was scared she had fallen down. I was surprised she could stand at all. I knocked again. "Mom, you okay?"

"Yes, Kimmi, I'm fine," she said, and opened the door, her face fresh and clean. She had a glow about her, an I-almost-died-and-saw-the-light glow. Even her turquoise necklace seemed to scream, "I'm alive."

"Wow, you look beautiful," I said.

"Thanks, Kimmi," she said, pulling me in for a hug.

"What happened?"

"I'm not sure what happened," she said, walking over to the edge of the bed and sitting down. "I was heading down headfirst being bounced like a rag doll off boulders. Mikey came in after me, screaming at me to swim. But I couldn't. I had swallowed too much water. I was too weak. I was dying. I was. I saw my friend Lucrezia in the sky. I saw my mother. And all I kept thinking was, *I can't die here in front of my children. I've just started to live.* Then Mikey screamed again, 'You better fucking swim or you're going to fucking die.' I had been clutching my paddle in one hand and my sunglasses in the other, and in that moment, I let go. Mikey caught up with me, grabbed my life vest and turned me around. I put my foot down, even though I wasn't supposed to, and got myself over to safety."

"I love you so much," I said, squeezing her hand, not able to fathom life without her.

Something shifted.

For the first time since the divorce, I was happy that she looked pretty and young. I was happy she was smiling. So what if she wanted to dance with a twenty-one-year-old? Or drink too much wine? Or swim drunk at 2 A.M.? God bless her.

★   ★   ★

Staring down at the river pictured to the right of the Empress's throne, I tell Iris, "I felt released from taking care of my mother when she saved herself during a river accident in Costa Rica. Well, my brother actually saved her, but her newfound will to live was a big part of it."

"And up until that point, *you* felt like the parent?" Iris says, her eyebrows furled, looking like a concerned schoolteacher's.

"My mother was a good mother," I say and cross my arms over my chest. "She loved us very much. She really did. She hugged and kissed us all the time. She made us healthy school lunches. No one ever wanted to trade with us, but they were healthy. She told us we could be anything we wanted to be. She listened to our stories. She was alwa—"

"I'm not knocking your mother," Iris says, putting out her hand to reassure me.

"I just feel defensive of her. She had a very rough childhood. She was sexually abused and beaten, and in some ways, she was just as much of a kid as Mikey and I were when we were growing up. I think she saw my dad as a father figure, and then over the years, she grew up and wanted out."

"That happens a lot," Iris says, and pauses. "The Empress uses the will and power of the Magician and the instincts and wisdom of the High Priestess to protect herself and her creations in the world. If a little girl is not protected by her mother, and later becomes a mother herself, she often does not have the necessary skills to protect her children. Only when she learns how to protect herself will her children feel safe. It's a cycle that's hard to break."

"My mother could have abused us, but she didn't. She was just very wounded."

"We're all wounded," Iris says. "That's what I was trying to say before, that we all have a dark side we bury that we then later have to deal with. There is a dark and light side with every card too, depending on how you read it. The mother archetype is complex. Like Mother Nature, she protects and destroys, she nurtures and swallows."

"Well, my relationship with my mother is certainly complex."

"The Empress is showing up in your difficulties in the past position," Iris says, taking the card back from me. "Which means you've mostly overcome your difficulties with your mother or she has overcome her difficulties with herself."

"It's amazing what she's survived in her life, what she keeps learning, how she keeps growing. One of the main reasons she got divorced was that she wanted to be a good example for us, to show us it's never too late to be happy or to love yourself, and then she loved herself a little too much," I say, and laugh.

"So now, when you have a child one day, you'll be able to continue the healing and change your family for generations to come."

La Muerte / La Mort
Arcana: XIII
Path on Kabbalah Tree of Life: 24
Color: Blue-Green
Astrological Sign: Scorpio
Constellation: Dragon of the Pole
Musical note: G

chapter six
death

"People living deeply have no fear of death."
—ANAÏS NIN

"Iris?"

"Yes, Kimberlee?

"What if I'm not ready to be a mother?"

"Then don't be a mother," she says as if it were as simple as choosing the French fries over the salad, which in my experience, actually, is not a simple decision.

"This whole time I've been focused on Noah not being ready, but I think I'm just as ambivalent. Maybe I picked someone who isn't ready to get married or have children because deep down I'm scared of getting divorced and screwing up my kids."

"Maybe. But let's say you got divorced and messed up your kids? So what?"

"So what? It'd be a disaster," I say, incredulous she could ask such a question.

"It would? Really? Are *you* a disaster? Is *your mother* a disaster?"

"No, but—"

"I'm not advocating going through life thinking it's all going to shit anyway, so why try?"

"Shit"? Did you just say "shit"? I've been trying to be so good all night.

"I'm saying if you put too much pressure on yourself to be perfect," Iris continues, "you'll end up hurting yourself. Or you'll become immobilized. You'll sit at home and wonder what your life would have been like if—"

"Okay, I get your point."

"Life is an adventure," Iris continues. "If you're afraid of doing it wrong, if you think of it as something you have to get through, then you'll create more suffering for yourself," she says, and hands me the next card, no setup, no explanation, no warning.

"Death?" I say, dropping it onto the table like a hot potato.

"That's what you get," Iris says as if she's punishing me.

"Well, it's not what I want. Can I pick another card?"

"No, this is what came up for you."

"Well, I don't want to die and I don't want anyone I know to die," I say.

"People who are scared of death are usually scared of life," Iris says, and hands me back the Grim Reaper.

*　*　*

It was November 1, 1997, the second night of the Day of the Dead. I was sitting by myself, eating spicy tortilla soup at one of the outdoor restaurants lining the Zócalo, the main square in the center of Oaxaca, Mexico, when I noticed a middle-aged couple staring at me as if I were a famous movie star they couldn't quite place.

"Whatchadoin' with such a fancy camera?" the man asked, pointing to the video camera sitting in my lap.

"Uh," I said. I was twenty-five, but looked and felt nineteen. It was the first time I had traveled by myself to a foreign country. I was nervous about everything. I placed my hand on my fanny pack and recited my practiced answer: "Well, I'm afraid of death, so I borrowed my friend's camera and came down here to make a documentary film about how other cultures handle it."

They burst into laughter.

"What's so funny? I really want to make documentaries. What's wrong with that?"

"No, that's great," the man said.

"We're sorry," the woman said.

"Listen," the man continued. "We've been coming to Oaxaca for years. Would you like to finish your soup over here? We can tell you all about the Day of the Dead."

They were wearing matching red Hawaiian shirts, which seemed odd, given we were in Mexico, but they didn't look like kidnappers, so I scooted up beside them and lapped up the rest of the spicy tomato broth as they told me how and why the locals celebrate death in the way that they do.

"Okay, first of all," the man said, motioning with his hand as if giving me the lay of the land, "*Día de los Muertos* is like visitation rites. It's the one time during the year that people can spend time with the deceased."

"Wait. Wait. Can I film this?" I asked.

"Sure," they said in unison.

I slipped the side strap of the camera onto my right hand, removed the lens cap and hit record with my thumb. "Okay, I'm rolling," I said, placing my eye to the camera to frame the shot. I felt so professional, although looking back, I'm pretty sure I looked ridiculous.

"Should I repeat that?" the man asked.

"Yes, if you could, please," I said, zooming in on his face.

"*Día de los Muertos* is like visitation rites. It's the one time during the year that people can spend time with the deceased," he said again.

"Wait. What are your names?" I asked, going back to a wide shot.

"Kathy," the woman said, fluffing up her long, ash-blond hair.

"Ray," the man said. "We've been coming here for years. We have a small business in Arizona where we sell Oaxacan black-on-black pottery."

He sounded like a used-car commercial.

"Oaxaca is a magical place," Kathy said. "And this is a really special festival. It's the one pagan holiday the locals were able to keep after Catholicism took hold. They merged it with All Souls' Day."

"Children's souls returned last night," Ray added.

"That's sad," I said.

"It's much sadder when people think they can never speak to their children again," Kathy said. "This is a way the living and the dead can stay connected."

"Tonight is when the adult souls return," Ray said.

"How do they return?" I ask.

"People lure their loved ones with elaborate altars, which act as landing pads, so the spirits can find their way home," Kathy said.

"And anyone can do this?" I asked.

"Do you know someone who has passed on?" she asked.

I turned off the camera and placed it back in my lap.

"Yeah, my mother's mother, my nana, died last year."

"You should create an altar for her," she said.

"Uh, I don't think so. We had a complicated relationship."

"You could make peace with her," Kathy said. "That's something the Day of the Dead is good for. It allows people resolution. You could go to the market down the street, over there," she said, and pointed. "Get *Pan de Muertos*, bread of the dead, candles, marigolds, calla lilies, chocolate— something you think might get her attention, her favorite candy, anything she would recognize."

"She liked saltwater taffy," I said.

"You're not going to find that here," Ray said.

And I'm not about to make an altar for my dead nana.

After thanking them and paying my check, I headed toward the market. On my way down the street, I passed children asking for money and wrinkled women selling bundles of gardenias for a peso. I turned on the camera. I needed good B-roll—shots of people and scenery, local flavor.

I held it as steady as possible and entered the market, filming aisles of fruit, vegetables, hanging slabs of meat, chickens that still needed to be plucked. The ceilings were low and the aisles were narrow. People were shoving past me, jolting my shot. I was starting to feel claustrophobic, lost in an intricate maze with no idea how to get out. Then I saw the flowers, hundreds of them sticking out of beat-up buckets. Golden yellow. Orange. White. I bought a few of each. Next to the flowers was the chocolate. I bought the kind shaped like a wheel with triangular bite-sized sections. Next to the chocolate were candles. It looked as if I was making an altar for my nana after all. All I needed was bread of the dead and I'd be good to go.

I stepped out of the market into the sun and saw the stand. There were fifty loaves stacked up high. They looked like round challahs. Each one had a little plastic face or skull sticking out of the top. I picked one with a skull.

I walked back to my room, tucked away in the far corner of the courtyard of Hostal de La Noria, and carefully placed each item on top of the dresser, trying to arrange everything artistically to make it look like an authentic altar, not that I had ever seen one. I placed the last piece of chocolate in front of the bread and stepped back to admire my work. Then I took out my camera and started filming.

As I stood there, scanning up and down the dresser, zooming in on the flickering candle, the room grew colder. I looked around. The fan was still on low. The window was open just a crack, the way I had left it. I turned off my camera and placed it on the bed. Something strange was going on. I peeked into the bathroom. No one was there. I looked under the bed. Nothing. And then I knew. My nana had found her way back. Her spirit was looming above me. All the blood in my body rushed to my feet. This wasn't good. I grabbed my jean jacket and camera and got the hell out of there.

The last time I had seen my nana was in a dream the night she died, before I knew she was dead. We had been estranged for years. I couldn't pretend what happened to my mother didn't happen or that my nana hadn't threatened to stop speaking to my mother if she ever told anyone. In the dream, my nana was wearing a light blue satin nightgown like the one she used to wear when she came to visit us in Tulsa. I loved my nana back then. Her long fingernails. Her high-pitched voice. The way she called my mother "Lori." She approached me with open arms in the dream. I told her I loved her and gave her a hug. When I woke up, I couldn't muster up anything for her. I didn't even cry when my mother broke the news.

I shut the door to my room and walked away quickly,

hoping my nana's spirit wasn't following me. It was dark. The streetlamps lit the way for people as they scurried in and out of restaurants and jumped on and off busses. I must have looked lost because an older man with white hair, crazy eyebrows and a lascivious twinkle in his eye, standing in front of a yellow school bus, looked at me and said in unaccented English, "Hey, Little Missy. Wanna hop on?"

I tried to ignore the innuendo.

"Where are you guys going?" I asked.

"We're off to the cemetery. It should be a good ol' time."

"I don't know," I said, and looked at the older women sitting in window seats.

Why not? What was I going to do? Go back to my hotel room and have it out with my nana?

"Ladies first," he said, holding out his arm.

"Okay," I said, and climbed onto the bus. I stood in the aisle, looking at all the faces staring up at me, feeling like a kid on her first day of school. Except this wasn't intimidating. They looked as if they might pee in their pants with excitement to have someone so young join them. I smiled and sat down in an empty seat toward the front, cradling my camera close to my chest.

"Mind if I take the window seat?" the man who invited me to join the group asked, motioning for me to get up so he could get in. "My name's Larry. What's with the camera?"

"Well, I came down here by myself to make a documentary film about how other cultures handle death." I left out the part about "being scared of death." I figured he had more to be scared of at his age than I did at mine.

"You're a brave young woman for coming to Mexico by yourself," the woman behind us said, moving to the aisle seat across from me. "I'm Emily."

"Nice to meet you, Emily," I said, looking into her eyes. They looked familiar. I thought my nana might have hijacked her body.

She reached over and held my hand. Her skin was cold and damp. I hated to admit it, but I was scared of old people too, who now seemed to be coming at me from all sides, like the bodies sprouting up from the ground in *Poltergeist*.

"You remind me of my granddaughter, sweet young thing," Emily said, and continued to hold my hand. "I never get to see her, though. I live in Florida and she lives in California." She paused and rubbed the top of my hand with her thumb. "You're making a film about death?"

"How did you know?" I asked, jumping back, letting go of her hand.

"I heard you tell Larry," she said, and laughed. "What are you finding so far?"

That if you make an altar for your dead nana, she'll swoop down and take over a nice old lady's body on a bus. "I met some people in the Zócalo earlier today who told me a little bit about the festival. They let me film them. Maybe I could interview you."

"Now? Isn't it too dark?"

"Yeah, we should wait."

When we arrived at the cemetery, it was burning bright, thousands of candles set off by bundles of calla lilies and marigolds piled up high on every gravesite. It looked as though the sky had fallen down and people were walking through rows of stars.

As we passed through the gates, I pressed record on my camera and kept it low by my hip. I didn't want to be obtrusive or disrespectful. These were people. Real people. Mothers, fathers, grandparents. People they had loved were buried in this ground, right here, under this earth. I rounded the corner and saw a man standing on top of an actual gravesite, setting up his tripod to get a shot with his Nikon. I suddenly didn't feel so bad. I shot him a dirty look and then noticed the red light on my camera had stopped blinking, which meant it wasn't recording, which meant it might be broken, which meant, omigod. Had I really broken my friend's $2,000 camera?!

Just then, Emily put her arm through mine as if we were a couple and asked me if I could help steady her walk. I wanted to say no. I was upset and needed to figure out what the hell was wrong with the camera. "Sure, Emily," I said, walking her through the rest of the cemetery, regretting my decision to get on the bus, regretting my decision to make my nana an altar, regretting my decision to talk to those death-crazed Arizona people, but most of all, regretting my decision to come down to Oaxaca in the first place.

An hour later, the bus dropped me off at my hotel and everyone waved good-bye from the windows. They had invited me to join them the next day, but I couldn't, I had to find someone who could fix my friend's camera.

I opened the door to my room and stepped inside. It smelled like sugar cookies. I placed my camera by the door and immediately started to disassemble the altar. I moved the flowers to the bathroom; I threw away the bread; I ate the chocolate; and I left the candles on the dresser. Then I took a shower, thinking the steam might melt away my nana's spirit like the Wicked Witch of the West.

Crawling into bed, I decided to read a book. I needed to calm down, but I couldn't concentrate. What if I couldn't get the camera fixed? How could I make a documentary film without a camera? What was I going to say to my friend? I put the book down and turned off the light. The ceiling fan made a weird noise. I turned the light back on. It reminded me of the time I had mice in my apartment. Every creak freaked me out. I drifted in and out of sleep all night, my eyes popping open and then closing again.

The next morning, I woke up early and tried to find a camera repair shop. I flipped through the phone book but couldn't find any listings that seemed appropriate. I asked the woman at the front desk. She had no idea what I was talking about. I didn't even know what was wrong with the thing. I walked around the empty, sleepy streets, looking for an open electronics shop, but it was a Sunday in a Catholic country, and All Souls' Day to boot. I was fucked.

I thought about Emily and Larry and the other old people on the bus and their invitation to join them. What else was I going to do? I wasn't about to hang out in my room all day. And walking around wasn't going to fix the camera.

I ran back to my room, hid the camera under the bed, changed out of ripped jeans and put on a green cotton dress covered with gold swirls.

When Emily saw me, her eyes widened with excitement. "I'm thrilled you came!"

"After you finish your eggs, we're off to the Mercado!" the tour guide screamed, her voice gravelly and eyes puffy, possibly still drunk from the night before.

Emily leaned in and whispered in my ear, "I'm sorry, but I promised Valerie I would sit with her today."

I was relieved. I didn't think I could handle an entire day of holding hands.

Everyone piled onto the bus. Larry. Emily. Valerie. The tour guide. An American woman I didn't recall seeing the night before, someone much younger than the rest of them. I decided to sit next to her.

"Hi, my name is Kimberlee," I said.

"I'm Rachel," she said, keeping her eyes on the road.

"What are you doing in Oaxaca?" I asked, trying to make conversation.

"I live in Puerto Vallarta. I'm visiting Sue, the tour

guide," she said, her eyes still straight ahead. Her permed blond hair and pink T-shirt seemed at odds with her impenetrable demeanor.

"Well, I came here to make a documentary film about death, well, documentary video, whatever, and then last night, my camera mysteriously stopped working and I couldn't find anyone to fix it this morning, and you can't make a film without a came—"

"It's Sunday. There's nothing you can do. Let it go."

But I couldn't let it go. And who was she to tell me what to do anyway?

"You're good at letting things go?" I asked, trying not to sound bitchy.

"Breast cancer puts things into perspective."

I swallowed hard and stared out the window for the rest of the ride.

We pulled into an outdoor market outside the city's center. The edible dried grasshoppers on display didn't strike anyone's fancy, so everyone just milled about, waiting to get back on the bus.

I looked over at Emily, who was arm in arm with Valerie, and noticed that she didn't look well. Her pale skin was becoming paler and her hands were starting to tremble. I wasn't sure what was wrong. She extended her free arm, as if trying to grab on to something, and then fell to the ground, wetting herself on the way down. Valerie, not strong enough to catch her, screamed out, "Help! We need help!"

I stood still and watched Emily's body continue to convulse. She looked like a fish on land gasping for water.

Luckily, there were several retired doctors in the group who crouched down beside her and checked her vitals.

After a few minutes, she stopped moving altogether.

"Someone call an ambulance," one of the men screamed to one of the Spanish vendors. *"AMBULANCIA!"*

Larry came up behind me and asked, "Where's your camera now?"

I flipped around.

"You wanted to learn about death," he said, raising his shoulders.

Was he fucking kidding me? Did he think I was a monster? That I would actually be shooting this?

I felt dizzy and spotted a nearby bench.

On my way over, Rachel reached out and touched my arm, looking me in the eyes for the first time all day. "It's okay."

I nodded, unable to speak or smile.

My breath was thick and heavy. I sat down on the cold cement seat and inhaled deeply. On my exhalation, I burst into tears. I didn't understand what was happening to me. Why was I so upset? I didn't know Emily. I hadn't cried for my nana when she died. Why was I crying for a total stranger?

I thought back to the altar and to Emily and her soft hands. *This* was what it felt like to be touched. I looked up at the Oaxacan sky and took another breath. My nana was with me. I could feel it.

death

I notice Iris has eaten away most of her red lipstick, now lining only the outer edges of her lips, exposing the pink, delicate, wrinkly flesh underneath. It makes her look vulnerable, although I'm pretty sure I'm the only one who feels vulnerable at this moment. I look down at Death and try to breathe.

The Grim Reaper is suited in black metal armor sitting on top of a white horse. The sun is rising in the distance. There's a priest praying, a woman fainting, a child kneeling, a waterfall falling, and a dead king who has lost his crown.

"Death represents transformation, a form of renewal," Iris says. "It signifies the death of something, not necessarily life. The death of an old way of being. The death of an idea. The death of a dynamic. The death of self. It represents profound, life-altering change."

"Can the actual death of a person be a catalyst for this kind of change?" I ask. "Because my nana's death totally transformed my mother. She was finally free to tell the truth. To be herself."

★   ★   ★

My mother, her half sister, my brother and I snuck into the lobby of the Plaza Hotel like bank robbers. Every eye in the room gravitated to my mother in her Doctor Zhivago black fur hat while the rest of us tried not to call attention to ourselves. The room was under my mother's name, so we waited by the elevator while she sashayed over to the front desk to get the key.

"Thank you, Tad. You're a doll," I heard her say. I was surprised she didn't fake a southern accent. She was very good at accents. She said that it was because she was musical and that people who are musical are also good with languages. I failed French and Spanish. She thanked Tad again and flipped her long, blond extensions in his face.

We followed her into the ornate elevator, but didn't dare say a word. We were still pretending to be strangers. When the four of us got off on the third floor, it may have looked suspicious, but the mother and daughter from Texas were too busy talking about their trip to FAO Schwarz to notice.

Suite 311 was all the way down the hall to the right. We stepped quietly, stealthily. I was pretty sure what we were about to do was illegal. My mother looked around one more time before opening the door.

Five hundred bucks for this?! We didn't need a big place; we weren't spending the night. But man, what a rip-off. It was maybe two hundred square feet. There was a queen-sized bed that took up most of the room, two cherry wood nightstands, a closet, a small bathroom with a shiny white porcelain tub, and a damask upholstered chair plucked from a Merchant Ivory film in the corner by the one measly window.

My aunt set up the guacamole and chips on one of the bedside tables. My brother opened the champagne and rounded up four glasses. And my mother took out the little Ziploc bag. I couldn't believe that this was all that was left of nana . . . a huge, looming presence in our lives reduced to what looked like New York City soot. My mother opened the bag and ran her fingers through her mother's ashes as if she were combing a beach. "It's chunkier than I thought it'd be," she said.

I held my breath, afraid of flying particles.

"You can't hold your breath forever, Kimmi," my mother said, still combing through the chunks.

I exhaled, rolled over to the other side of the bed and grabbed a glass of champagne.

My brother was crawling around on the floor, looking for a good place to put her. "Hey, look at this, it's a non-working vent! This is perfect! Do you guys have a screw-driver?"

Luckily for my brother, my mother had a Swiss Army knife on her.

I got up and examined the bedposts. "What about these? Look, they unscrew." I wanted to trump my brother.

"That's great, Kimmi. She'd be very happy to be in the bed," my mother said.

My nana had spent the last few years of her life bedridden with rheumatoid arthritis, living in a prefab home in Northern California, watching Regis and Kathie Lee until the very end. She had been dirt poor her entire life and had always envied the rich, so it wasn't entirely surprising that her last wish was to be scattered in the fanciest hotel in New York City.

I asked if anyone happened to bring rubber gloves. I

was out of luck. I held the bag carefully, trying not to spill anything onto the floor or my hand, and poured some ashes down the bedpost.

My brother turned on the radio.

Give me the beat boys and free my soul

"Mom, didn't you think it was 'Give me the beach boys?'" I asked.

"I'd take a beach boy any day of the week," my mother said, and laughed. "Now get back to work."

My mother wanted us to find as many out-of-reach places as we could to guarantee her mother wouldn't be swept away or vacuumed up.

My brother was winning. So far, he had found the vent, a bathroom sconce, a hole in the dresser and a nook in the windowsill.

I excused myself to the bathroom to wash my hands. I turned on the hot water and scrubbed my skin hard. What were we doing here? Was this honoring her life? Had my mother really forgiven her?

When I came out, my mother was crying.

I sat down on the bed next to her and held her hand, even though I was scared my nana's ashes would stick to my skin. "I can't believe she's gone," she sobbed. "My mommy is gone."

I thought back to a story someone told me about a little girl whose mother had burned her with a hot iron, sending her to the hospital with third-degree burns. The girl was in excruciating pain, facing multiple skin grafts, but kept calling out for her mother, the woman who had hurt her so badly.

A few hours later, the chips were gone, the guacamole was crusty, and there were no more places to put my nana, so we said good-bye and shut the door.

THE DEVIL.

El Diablo / Le Diable
Arcana: XV
Path on Kabbalah Tree of Life: 26
Color: Blue-Violet
Astrological Sign: Capricorn
Constellation: Goat and Coachman
Musical note: A

chapter seven
the devil

"Hell is empty and all the devils are here."
—WILLIAM SHAKESPEARE

"Transformation and change come in many forms. Sometimes someone has to die for us to be free. Other times, we hold the key to our imprisonment," Iris says, and hands me the next card.

I look down and see two people chained to a hairy-ass devil. "This is the key to my imprisonment?" I ask. "An S and M version of the Lovers card?"

"Into whips and chains, are we?" Iris says, and smiles.

"No, I'm not. But look at this," I say, and point, as if she hasn't seen the card a million times. "The man and woman are in the same position as the Lovers, except now they have chains around their necks, horns on their heads, and tails. And instead of an Angel overhead, there's a mean-looking Devil making the Heil Hitler sign."

"Or maybe he's just waving hello."

"Maybe," I say, staring at the vine of grapes attached to the woman's ass.

"People think the Devil is evil, when really, he explores things we're taught to *view* as evil or shameful, like sex, unbridled desires, excess, obsession. Just as Death transforms us, the Devil also transforms us, using negativity as a transformer."

"How can negativity be a good thing?"

"The Devil forces us to acknowledge our dark side. When we take things out of the shadows and bring them to the surface, we can begin the integration process and become whole again, like the Lovers, so it's actually not a coincidence that the cards look alike."

"Why are all my cards pointing to my darkness? Is that normal? I mean, what about other people? Do they get the same kind of thing?"

"Everyone has to deal with their darkness. These cards speak to everyone, but in different ways. Your darkness is different from mine, different from your mother's."

"When you say darkness, are you talking about badness?"

"Some call it bad. Some call it evil. Good girl. Bad girl. I'm a saint. You're a whore. When we judge ourselves and others in these terms, we get into trouble."

★   ★   ★

Jason's breathing was heavy and short. My ear was pressed so hard against the phone, I could practically feel his body on the other end. I wondered if he was stroking his penis, or, as he liked to call it, his "cock." Jason loved the word "cock." He was dirty. Not in a homeless-guy-masturbating-on-the-street kind of way. More in an I'll-slap-you-on-the-ass-and-you'll-like-it kind of way.

"Why don't I come over there and make you a bad little girl?" he said. "You wanna be a bad girl, don't you?"

Every cell in my body wanted to scream, "Yes! Come over here right now and make me a bad girl!"

But Jason was married.

We had met at a mutual friend's party and spent the whole night in a corner talking. When he looked at me, I felt beautiful and sexy, which at the time felt more powerful than the gold band on his ring finger. A month later, what had been innocent flirting turned into heavy breathing over the phone on a Sunday afternoon.

It was June 7, 1998, and the first time in four years since Zach and I had broken up that I felt something, anything, for anyone.

"Jason—" I started to say.

"Yes?" he said, panting like a dog.

"I really want love."

"And you're really no fun," he said, and hung up the phone.

That was it.

I wanted to kick myself. Why couldn't I let myself be a

bad girl? I could be a bad girl. I could embrace my inner whore, goddammit.

I reached under my bed, grabbed my back massager and turned it on the lowest speed. I closed my eyes and imagined what it would have been like if I had said yes, if he had come over. I could feel his strong hands on my breasts and smell the mustiness of his sweat. . . .

The next morning, I was at work, slumped down in my chair, watching *The View.* It was a slow news day. No affiliate live shots. An occasional fiber feed to book, but that only took a minute. Karen, who sat two feet to my left, was checking her astrology again, and Gary, who sat two feet to my right, was listening to CNN.

The phone rang. "Live Desk, Kimberlee speaking," I answered.

"Kimmi, Kimmi, Kimmi. I met a man!" my mother sang.

"That's great," I said, cringing.

"Shirley met him at a party in the Hamptons and thought he was my type, and boy oh boy, is he ever! He lives in the city. He's a professor at The New School. His name is Biiiiiiiiiiiill and he is deeeelicious!" she squealed as if she were about to throw pom-poms into the air and do the splits.

"That's great," I said.

Shirley was an artist and one of the few friends my mother got to keep after the divorce; my father got most of them. Shirley was blond like my mother, and they both still wore 80s-style frosted pink lipstick, making them look like the Barbie I liked to take to the beach when I was a little girl.

"Shirley found someone for you too."

"Mom, really, that's okay. Thanks."

"His name is Marco. He's single. He's a Jewish painter from Argentina. Who knew there were Jewish painters in Argentina? Anyway, he's staying with her for the summer. Some kind of apprenticeship. Supposedly, he is hot, hot, hot."

I thought back to what Jason had said to me on the phone: "You're no fun." Where was my sense of fun? What would be so bad about meeting Marco? At least he wasn't married.

"Okay, Mom. Set it up."

It was about time for *me* to be the girl-gone-wild.

"Just like that? Are we loosening up in our old age?"

"Twenty-six is not that old, thank you very much."

"My baby is becoming a woman," she said, as if dating a foreigner were a prerequisite for womanhood.

Two weeks later, my mother and I climbed into her white Mercedes convertible, the one she bought on eBay with her divorce settlement. Ever since the split, my mother had become addicted to two things: men and the Internet. Bad combination.

As we made our way out to the tip of Long Island, I stayed away from topics I knew would upset me: what had gone wrong with my father . . . how much she liked Bill . . . what she liked to do with Bill. Basically, everything she wanted to talk about. It was easier to just eat and sing, so I turned up the radio and handed her a sourdough pretzel. The Divinyls song "I Touch Myself" came on. I rolled my eyes as my mother belted it out like a porn star.

When we pulled up to the gallery, my palms started to sweat. I checked my face nervously in the visor mirror before getting out of the car. My hair was tied in a medium-high ponytail and my bangs hung down over my eyebrows. I wasn't wearing much makeup, just lip gloss and bronzer. Next to my mother in her cleavage-exposing turquoise top, I looked like an angel in my white cotton peasant blouse.

"Come on, Kimmi," my mother said, opening the car door and getting out.

I stayed seated. I couldn't move.

She walked over to my side of the car and knocked on the window. "Let's go," she said, and tapped on her Cartier watch. "Today."

Something about the way she said "today" pissed me off. I wanted to outdo her. Outshine her. Show her that I, too, could conquer men.

I walked into the gallery wagging my hips a little wider than usual.

Shirley rushed over to us in all her four foot eight, double-D glory and reached up on her tippy-tip-toes to hug us.

My mother whispered in Shirley's ear, "Bill is the best! Thank you."

"I knew you'd like him," Shirley whispered back. Then she looked my way and giggled. "Now it's your turn."

My feet wouldn't move.

"Are you coming?" she asked, reaching out her hand for me.

I couldn't open my mouth.

"Someone's being a little shy?" she asked my mother. "Marco!" she yelled out, and gestured for him to come over.

He was bent down, sliding one of his paintings out of a crate. He looked up and over. My knees melted. I was staring at the girl from Ipanema's long-lost brother. He was tall, dark and handsome, and I knew I was in over my head. My face flushed and I looked at the floor. I could see his hairy legs approaching us. He was wearing cut-off jean shorts, which usually make a man look gay or like he stepped out of a *Playgirl* spread, but for some reason, they just made him look hotter.

I couldn't breathe.

"*Hola.*"

Looking into his eyes, I had a flash of him riding a motorcycle without a helmet on a dirt road just outside of Buenos Aires eating a jalapeño pepper without flinching.

"Do you speak English?" I asked, not knowing what else to say.

"*Poco.*"

"I can say, '*Café con leche, por favor.*'"

"*Bueno.*"

I felt stupid and racist. I wasn't treating him like the man who could rock my world, but like a man who could make me a latte.

He nodded, smiled and walked away.

This wasn't going well.

I walked around the gallery, admiring some of Shirley's sculptures, and watched Marco unpack the rest of his paintings. He was bent over again, tearing cardboard, ripping off tape, his cut muscles bulging.

"Let's head to the house," my mother said, tapping me on the shoulder, smiling.

Later that night, I was standing at Shirley's sink, deveining shrimp, my hands covered with fleshy remains, looking out at the sun setting over the choppy water. My mother and Shirley were sitting on the white couch in the living room sipping wine and talking about Bill, I imagined. Marco was in his room. I was in my own little world, the song "May This Be Love" by Jimi Hendrix ringing through my head. "Waterfall. Nothing can harm me at all." I was back in Denver with Zach, sitting in his burgundy Honda, looking out at the blazing fluorescent sunset falling over the Rocky Mountains.

"Kimmi, that's not how you clean shrimp," my mother said, pushing me aside. "Watch me do it." She grabbed a shrimp. "See. You take it," she said, and inserted the deveiner into the middle of the shrimp. "Then in one fluid movement, you remove the vein without shredding the shrimp into pieces."

Ever since Japan, shrimp had skeeved me out. I began to feel sick to my stomach. "I'll be right back," I said, and went outside onto the deck to catch the last rays of sun. If I were more like my mother, I wouldn't be scared of shrimp.

I would have made my move on Marco already. I'd be tossing my hair in his face instead of daydreaming about my ex-boyfriend. My mother knew how to work men like no one else in the world. Who was I kidding? I didn't want to work men. I wanted to love one man. I wanted to feel the way I had felt in Zach's car.

"Dinner's ready," my mother yelled out through the sliding-glass door screen.

I turned around, half expecting her to be dressed in a blue velour robe like the one she used to wear on Taco Night when I was a kid. I wanted to be back there, but I wanted "back there" to be different. I wanted my parents to like each other, so they'd never get a divorce. I wanted my brother to be healthy. I wanted to feel safe.

"You were out there a long time," my mother said, sounding pissed off that I'd left her to clean the rest of the shrimp.

"I'm sorry. I needed some air."

I was disappointing her—I could feel it. I poured myself a glass of wine.

Marco waited for us to start and then positioned his knife in his right hand and his fork in his left hand, placing his pointer finger on the top of each utensil as he gently cut his shrimp into two pieces and took a bite. I was expecting him to be more sensual. I thought he'd eat with his hands and lick his fingers clean.

My mother asked him how he liked Argentina and then started to sing "Don't Cry for Me, Argentina," telling him that *Evita* was her favorite musical. He nodded politely

155

and looked at me. His look entered me. It felt hard and forceful, and I blushed.

After dinner, I cleaned the dishes while Marco set up his projector. My mother had been bugging him about it all night. "I'd love to see your art. Show us your art."

The first slide was a painting of five vintage cars lined up on a tropical island road. Wow. He was good. Really good. Beautifully balanced composition. Surprising light play. And rich use of color—mustards and lush greens. I was no art critic, but this stranger with a golden tan and reluctant smile was the real deal. I wanted to feel him inside me, and knew my mother would be proud. With every click of a slide, my desire for him grew. Combed white-sand beaches, Old World blue and white-striped cabanas, teal-blue waters, then a stunning dark brown woman smiling in ecstasy, holding a ripe, juicy papaya. Her expression was so vibrant and alive; she jumped off the wall. I gasped. He was GAUGUIN!

Just then, he caught my eye and mouthed, *"Baño?"*

Baño? Bathroom! My high school Spanish was finally good for something.

As I walked him down the hallway, I could practically feel the heat emanating from his body. I pointed to the bathroom, accidentally touching his arm with my hand. I wanted to keep my arm in the air to touch his skin a little longer, but I turned around to go. He grabbed my hand, yanked me inside the bathroom, shut the door, put his hand in between my legs and asked, "Jes?"

"YES!" I said without flinching. I had no idea what I was agreeing to, but I didn't care. "Now?" I asked.

"Esta noche," he said, waving his hand to indicate "later."

"Here?" I asked, wondering if he wanted me to meet him back in the bathroom. He pointed down the hall to his bedroom. His bedroom! I had forgotten he had been living there for a week already. He knew where the bathroom was all along. Duh. I totally fell for it.

We slipped back into the living room as if he hadn't just put his hand on my vagina. Marco finished up the slide show. We drank a few more glasses of wine and then said good night. Shirley kissed us all on the cheek. Marco waved to my mother and me as we ascended the stairs to the bedroom we were sharing.

"Mom, Marco wants to have sex with me," I whispered as I closed the door behind us.

"That's great!" she said, reached into her purse and handed me a condom.

"What the hell?"

"I like to be prepared for life's little surprises."

I waited an hour or so until I thought Shirley had fallen asleep, and tiptoed back downstairs to Marco's room. I was going to fuck Gauguin! I brought along the condom my mother had given me, but didn't want to look presumptuous, so I placed it on the floor and knocked softly. When he didn't answer, I opened the door and slowly stepped inside.

Marco was sprawled out on the bed, naked, fresh out of the shower, his chest hair still full of droplets. I felt silly in my pink polka-dot pajamas. He looked me up and down and waved me over to the bed. Then he grabbed my arm and pulled me on top of him. It was all happening so fast. He had taken off my pajama top and bottoms and rolled on a condom from the bedside table drawer before I had the chance to say hello.

So much for foreplay.

As he climbed on top of me, I thought, this is my big moment, my chance to be a bad girl! I wanted to say, "My pussy is so wet for you," or "Fuck me from behind," or *"Café con leche, conquistador."* Instead, I said, "I don't sleep around. Really, I don't."

"Ju joke?"

"No, really, I don't do this."

"Ju like?"

I could hear my father's voice in my head: "Make sure men respect you. Don't let them use you." My mother's voice chimed in, "Sex is beautiful. Do what makes you feel good. You're the one who has to wake up the next morning and look at yourself in the mirror."

In.

Out.

In.

Out.

Marco's face contorted in the most unappealing way when he came. I didn't say anything dirty. My wild child made no appearance at all.

As I tiptoed back upstairs, I imagined what my mother would have done with Marco. She probably would have had five orgasms and shown him some crazy position out of the Kama Sutra. I opened the door. My mother's face looked peaceful, beautiful. I took a deep breath and thought, *I should really take a shower before getting back into bed with her.*

The next morning, I looked at myself in the mirror and felt surprisingly fine. So what if I didn't get down and dirty? I had a one-night stand with a hot Argentine painter. That was something.

My mother teased me on the ride back to the city. "You didn't even have an orgasm?"

I wished she were in therapy.

The next week, I was sitting on my bed in my studio apartment looking at the royal blue walls, wondering if light yellow would be better, when the phone rang. It was Marco. Shirley must have given him my number.

"I come visit? Jes?"

"YES!"

It was fun saying yes.

Maybe this one-night stand would turn into full-blown love. Maybe he was the one!

When the buzzer rang a few days later, I jumped to my feet, rushed to the door and threw my arms around him like they do in the movies. I wished he had spun me around, but he was wearing a large, overstuffed backpack and carrying an enormous portfolio—and I'm no waif.

I helped him with his things and offered him a drink.

"*¿Comida?*" he asked, sniffing the air.

Comida? Food! I was getting good at this Spanish thing.

I had spent the afternoon preparing salmon steaks, sautéed Swiss chard and steamed brown rice. I wanted something delicious to offer my new man.

We ate in silence. He kept nodding his head and smiling. I was glad he liked it. It was the only thing other than pasta I knew how to cook. We ate some more while I waited for more nods and smiles . . . and for our love to grow.

Nothing much happened.

He cleaned the dishes. I put on my cotton floral nightgown and crawled into bed. Marco climbed in after me and turned off the light. We were lying next to each other, both on our backs, staring up at the ceiling. He gently placed his right hand on my stomach.

"Marco, I'm sorry. I have my . . . my . . . how do you say?"

He got the point and kissed me on the forehead. "*Buenas noches,* Kimberlee."

I turned over on my side and studied his profile in the dark. His nose was large and prominent. His eyebrows were full. They stuck out too. I wanted to talk to him, to find out about his family, but unfortunately, I didn't have a glow-in-the-dark Spanish dictionary. His breathing slowly changed into sleep breathing. Then he started to snore. I couldn't fall asleep. Who was this man? And why was he scratching himself?

The next morning, Marco woke up before I did. I cracked my eyes open and saw him standing in the kitchen, which was less than twelve feet away from the bed, making breakfast. I smiled and said in a sleepy voice, "*Bue . . . nos . . . no . . . ches,*" stretching my arms out like a cat. "*Tar . . . des . . . días. Buenos días.*"

He laughed and motioned me over to the couch, where he handed me a plate of the fluffiest eggs I had ever seen. I took one bite and swooned. Fluffy. Spicy. Perfect. I kissed him on the cheek and thanked him, "*Muchas gracias, Marco.*"

"Welcome, ju are, Kimberlee," he said.

Then he walked over to my sneakers, picked them up and threw them at me. I guessed we were going for a walk. He was already dressed and ready to go, so I threw on shorts and a T-shirt and followed him out the door. When the elevator opened to the lobby, Marco started to sprint to Riverside Park. I guessed we were going for a run.

My stomach was bloated and bouncing. My cramps were getting worse with each step. And my skin itched from all the blood circulating in places I wasn't used to feeling. I didn't want to seem like a baby or appear out of shape, which I was, so I ran alongside him without complaining, huffing and puffing the whole way.

Back at my place, Marco kissed my sweaty neck and grabbed my ass. I looked at the clock. It was 9 A.M. Shit. I was late for work.

I jumped in the shower and got dressed in ten minutes flat. "I'll meet you back here later tonight," I said, and then showed him how to lock the door behind him. "You push—" Marco took my hand and pulled me close. "I have to go to work, Marco. I'll see you tonight," I said, kissing him on the lips and twirling out of his arms like Ginger Rogers.

As I walked to work, I couldn't stop smiling. Peter Gabriel's "Salisbury Hill" was playing on my cassette Walkman and I could feel my heart soar.

"You sure seem happy today," the receptionist remarked as I walked into the office.

"I am!" I chirped back.

When I got to my desk, I threw my bag under my chair and started to daydream. Karen was multitasking, checking her email and watching one of the morning shows. Gary was listening to CNN as always. I just sat there, imagining what it would be like to marry Marco, to move to South America and become a flamenco dancer. In my head I was stomping my feet and clinking my castanets when my vagina started to itch. I looked around the newsroom to make sure no one was looking and scratched hard, then went back to South America in my mind. Would we live in a house with turquoise-painted shutter windows? My vagina was still itchy. I looked around one more time and scratched again. It didn't help, so I went to the bathroom, locked myself in one of the stalls and scratched my crotch like crazy.

Maybe I had a yeast infection? It *was* summertime.

Then I remembered that Marco had been scratching his pubic hair the night before.

I pulled down my skirt and underwear and searched through my pubic hair.

"OMIGOD, I see something!"

"Excuse me, are you okay in there?"

"Yeah, yeah, yeah. Everything's fine. Thanks."

My hands were shaking, but I managed to pick a tiny gray-brown spec off my skin with my fingernails and put it on a piece of toilet paper. I lifted it to my eyes to get a better look. *Ewww!* Were those legs?

I felt faint and sick to my stomach. I folded the toilet paper into a small square so no one would see it in my hand and walked back to my desk, trying to act calm. I didn't tell my boss I was leaving. I didn't say anything to Karen or Gary. I just grabbed my purse and left. When I got to the street, I bolted. I was becoming quite the runner.

Holding my little crab in one hand, completely out of breath, I stood at the pharmacy counter, unable to speak. I was too mortified to utter the word "crab" to the pharmacist, so I asked for a piece of paper and a pen and wrote him a note: "I think I have crabs. Please help me."

The pharmacist took me aside, looked me up and down and asked, "Have you been hiking? Maybe it's a tick?"

"I don't think so," I said, unfolding the piece of toilet paper and showing him the crab. He backed away slowly, but politely, and pointed to where I could find Nix Shampoo for head and pubic lice.

I bought two boxes and ran home.

When I got back to my apartment, I jumped in the shower and poured an entire bottle of Nix onto my body. I scrubbed and scrubbed and then shaved off all of my pubic hair. Then I ran downstairs to the laundry room, threw my

clothes and sheets into the big washer and washed everything in hot, hot water, even the colors. When I was done
with that, I ran back upstairs and vacuumed my rug. I spent
the rest of the afternoon shell-shocked, sitting on the edge
of the couch, waiting for Marco to come back from gallery
hopping with his portfolio.

Finally, the buzzer rang.

I jumped to my feet, opened the door and launched
into him before he even got inside. "You gave me crabs!"

"*¿Qué?*" he said, playing dumb.

How could he not have known?

"You gave me crabs!" I said again, my voice getting
louder.

"*No comprendo.*"

Inside the box there was a pamphlet written in English
and Spanish, so I took it out and held the Spanish side to
his face. "*¿Habla español?* Crabs!"

He read the sheet and then slowly pulled down his
pants and boxers.

We gasped at the same time.

He was crawling with crabs! Crawling.

"Eeeeewww, get in the shower right now," I screamed.

He washed and shaved everything off too, and then we
went downstairs to do *his* laundry. As he was loading his
clothes into the washer, I looked at him with a combination of disgust and sympathy. "Marco, you can't stay with
me anymore. I'm sorry, but I've heard it's possible that if
one little crab stays, you can be reinfested and reinfested,
and I'm not taking that chance with you. I'm just not. You

can't stay." I wasn't sure if he understood me, but then I saw tears well up in his eyes and knew he got it.

"But ju are special. We are special."

I don't give a shit, Gauguin. You're outta here.

★ ★ ★

"I tried to be a 'bad girl' once," I say to Iris. "I was so desperate to be like my mom, to be sexy and wild, not attached to love, that I had a one-night stand. Well, it was kind of a one-night stand. Anyway, the Universe punished me by giving me crabs."

"I'm fairly certain the *Universe* didn't give you crabs," Iris says, stifling a laugh.

"It was really gross."

"I'm sure it was, but what did you *learn* from it?"

"Uh, not to have sex with artists from Argentina."

"Kimberlee, Kimberlee, Kimberlee. What am I going to do with you?"

"You sound like my mom."

"Well, it's frustrating. You think if you do *this*, then you're good. If you do *that*, then you're bad. It's not that simple. Who decides what's good or bad anyway? Society? Religion? Your mother? The Devil card is about letting go of judgment and finding your authentic being."

"Are you trying to tell me getting crabs was a good thing?" I ask.

"No, Kimberlee. I'm not. But it taught you that following your truth is important. We all need to find what feels good and bad to us."

"Yeah, well, getting crabs definitely felt bad."

"Listen. We already know, based on the other cards that have come up tonight, that your mother's influence over you has been profound. You spent your life trying to protect her. When she was with your father, she was meek and surrendered her power. When she got divorced, she went wild. She had to strike her own balance, find what was right for her. We often try to emulate our parents. Maybe you thought that being more like your mother would make you happy."

"It didn't."

"It didn't. Exactly," Iris says, shaking her head up and down. "This card, in this position, represents a bridge to your current life, which makes sense. You needed to start looking at what was right and wrong for *you*. Your mother's journey is your mother's journey. And your journey is yours."

THE TOWER.

La Torre / La Tour
Arcana: XVI
Path on Kabbalah Tree of Life: 27
Color: Red
Planet: Mars
Constellation: Scorpion, Ophiuchus
Musical note: C

the tower

"Truths that wake, to perish never."
—WILLIAM WORDSWORTH

"Kimberlee, you're not going to like this," Iris says, handing me the next card fast, as if she were ripping off a Band-Aid.

I feel my face get sunburn-hot, only I'm not in the sun; I'm sitting in an old lady's apartment on a Sunday night, afraid to look at a stupid piece of paper.

"Go on," Iris urges me. "It's not going to bite. Its influence has already passed through your life. It could show up again, of course, you know, the cyclical nature of life, as we were discussing before. But this position indicates your recent past. The good news is that whatever it was is now over."

What's the bad news?

"Kimberlee, you're much stronger than you think."

My eyes fixate on the porcelain clock standing upright on the mantel. It's 11:11. I close my eyes. *I wish that . . . Noah and I get married . . . I find inner peace and the strength to stop picking my skin . . . and I think I might want to lose weight, ten pounds, maybe fifteen.* It's the same wish at 11:11 in the morning and at 11:11 at night. Every time the clock turns 11:12, I regret not wishing for World Peace and health for everyone on the planet. I open my eyes and see Iris looking at me. "I'm sorry," I say, pointing to the clock. "I had to make a wish. Well, actually, wishes. Plural. I always make several wishes when it turns 11:11."

"But it's 23:11," Iris says.

"Yeah, I know. We use military time at work, so I should know better, but whenever I see all those ones, I make a wish. It's a ritual. You know what's weird about it? I happen to look at the clock at this exact moment every day. Isn't that cool?"

"What would be *cool* is if you were to look at that card in your hand, so we're not here until 11:11 tomorrow," Iris says with a lift of her eyebrows.

"Fine, I'll look at the card I'm 'not going to like,'" I say, tensing my muscles as if I were about to jump off the high dive.

I see a burning tower, a woman and man falling to their deaths, the fear in their faces, orange and yellow flames.

the tower

Is this a cruel joke? This is the last thing any New Yorker wants to see.

I take a deep breath. "When I walked in here tonight, I had hope," I say, trying to choose my words carefully. "I don't know why, but I thought you would tell me everything was going to be okay. That Noah and I would get married. Have a happy life together. That my career would finally kick into gear. That my life would end up counting somehow." I pause, again trying to find the right words. "I know you don't believe in reading the future. I know that's not how you work, and you've been helpful. Really. I had no idea I had to address my 'darkness' to the extent you're telling me, or rather, these cards are telling me. I know *everyone* has to deal with their darkness, but the cards I keep getting are just so negative, devoid of all hope. I can't take it. First Death, then the Devil. Now a September 11 card?"

"I assure you, there is a light at the end of the tunnel," Iris says, and straightens her spine as if she were on a podium, about to speak to a crowd of three hundred people. "The Tower card, like September 11, seems to come out of nowhere, surprising us, shocking us out of our complacency. It represents the destruction of falsehood. It blows apart delusions and false comforts. We, as Americans, felt impervious to the terrors of the world for a long time. September 11 forced us to look at ourselves. In my opinion, we missed the opportunity the Tower card affords us. We could have rebuilt and reshaped with truth and integrity. Instead, our government stooped to an eye for an eye, or worse, someone else's eye for an eye, and as Gandhi said, 'An eye for an eye makes the whole world blind.'" Iris takes a breath to calm herself. "Getting off my soapbox, I will simply say that when the Tower passes through our lives, we often feel regret, regret for the choices we have made and the lies we have told ourselves."

★   ★   ★

It was Saturday and I was late for a dinner party. Holding a grocery bag from Fairway filled with olives, hummus, crusty bread and several bottles of Chimay beer, I flew down the subway stairs to catch the #1 train. When I reached the bottom step, I was struck by the sight of him. If I had been a cartoon character, my eyes would have popped out of my eye sockets on springs and the word "Wowza" would have been written in bubble letters above my head.

I tried to act cool and walked over to the don't-go-beyond-this-point, yellow edge of the platform. I placed my Fairway bag down and leaned over to see if the train was coming. I felt his presence next to me, but I ignored him the way I would a celebrity, not wanting to give in to my screaming-girl impulse. I looked at my watch, exhaled and fiddled with one of my braids. I had braided my hair into two braids, making me look as though I should be yodeling on the top of the Swiss Alps. Then I did the thing I did not want to do. I glanced over at him.

I tried to turn my eyes away, but they wouldn't budge. He was wearing a beige Burberry raincoat and looked like a model with his sandy, shaggy hair, bright green eyes and strong jaw line. There was something magnetic about him, regal almost. He stood tall and proud, head slightly lifted, as if he were too good to consort with the masses. He didn't make eye contact with anyone either, not the squat woman standing to his right trying to get something out of her ear, not the man with the dreads directly in front of him. He didn't seem to notice me either.

White light started to stretch across the tunnel tiles. The #1 train was coming.

The doors opened directly in front of me. I stepped aside to let the people off and then scurried aboard. I found an open seat and sat down next to a woman wearing a black skirt suit. I positioned the bag in between my legs so no one would squish my hummus, and looked up, hoping Burberry boy had picked the same subway car. And there he was . . . ten feet away, holding on to one of the metal handles, swaying back and forth to the movement of the train.

The doors opened and closed at Sixty-sixth Street. People shuffled off. Others pushed their way on. He was still standing. When the doors opened at the next stop, the woman next to me got up. I saw the color beige approaching. Burberry boy was sitting down. He was sitting down next to *me*. *Omigod.* In one second, we would be touching, touching the way strangers on subways touch. I held my breath and sucked in my stomach.

It was May 1, 1999, eight years since I had lost my virginity and almost five years since Zach and I had broken up for good. In that time, I had become a little too close to my "back massager," flirted way too heavily with a married man and gotten crabs from an Argentine painter. I was starting to think I would never have a boyfriend again, as if there were a shelf life to being available, and past a certain point, you go sour and get thrown out.

Sitting next to this gorgeous stranger, I had the urge to rest my head on his shoulder. I refrained.

Fiftieth Street was approaching, the place I got off weekday mornings to go to work. I had left Worldwide Television News in 1997 and had been at Fox News Channel for a little over a year and a half. I had already weathered the Monica Lewinsky scandal, Chris Farley's death and the Columbine school shootings. I hadn't been there long enough to hate it yet, but working in a basement was starting to get to me.

The train skidded to a stop. The doors opened. *Please, please don't get off, please don't get off.* He stayed seated. *Thank God.* His body was still next to mine. I wondered how much time we had left together, what he did for a living, if he was single, when someone on the train farted. We both started to laugh. That's all it took. A fart.

"Wanna switch cars?" he asked me, holding his nose, staring down at his feet.

"I think I'm okay," I said, laughing.

"Where you headed?" he asked.

"A friend's dinner party downtown. And I'm totally

late. I did the Revlon Walk for Women today and everything took longer than I thought it would," I said, pointing to the olives.

"I'm heading downtown too," he said. "I need to pick up a projector for a meeting on Monday. I just started my own company."

An entrepreneur? Sexy.

We continued to talk, but by the time we got to Fourteenth Street, we still didn't know each other's names. My stop, Houston, was coming up fast. *Please ask for my name and number.* Then, without warning, the train started to run express. It whizzed by Christopher Street, then Houston, Canal and Franklin, before it stopped at Chambers.

"Shit. Did I miss the announcement?"

"Don't worry," he said. "This is my stop. I'll find you a cab."

I liked his confidence and chivalry, so I followed him off the train.

"What's your name, by the way?" I asked.

"What do you think it is?"

"Uh, I don't know," I said.

"Guess, he said."

"Xander?"

"Who names their kid Xander? Daniel. It's Daniel. What's yours?"

"Kimberlee. With two 'e's," I said.

"Got an email address, Kimberlee with two 'e's?" he asked, whipping out his PalmPilot, a gadget I had never seen before.

"I actually just set up a Hotmail account last week," I said, and spelled out the address for him as we walked.

"Welcome aboard," he said, writing my email address on a screen with a plastic pen. "It's a stylus," he said, without looking up.

When we got to the corner, he hailed me a cab.

"Well, it was nice to meet you, Kimberlee," he said, holding out his hand. "I'm sure I'll see you again."

His handshake was strong—not too strong—and long, but not too long. It was perfect. My father always said you could tell a lot about a man by his handshake.

Daniel opened the door for me with his left hand and extended his right arm, as if to say, "Madame, your carriage awaits."

I got into the cab, shut the door and squealed. Inside, I was still a twelve-year-old girl.

"You okay back there?" the driver asked.

"Yeah, sorry. Houston and Thompson, please," I said, my voice still in its highest register.

I stared out the window and watched the sky open up. The buildings were still tall, the streets were still crawling with people, but something in my heart felt expansive, boundless. I couldn't believe it. I had met "the one" on the #1 train. The Universe hadn't forgotten about me after all.

The next day, I checked my email.

Nothing.

The day after that, nothing.

The third day, I saw his name!

I sprung out of my chair and did a little dance, arms churning imaginary butter, "He emailed me. He emailed me. He emailed me." Then I did the *Flashdance* run-in-place move and sat back down to read what he wrote:

I'm not in the habit of meeting people on the subway. It was nice. What's your deal? —D

I clicked reply. I wanted to sound breezy, but wasn't sure what to say. I didn't want to tell him that he had just met his future wife. I didn't want to tell him that I had already had two sexual dreams about him. And there was no way I was going to tell him I hadn't had a boyfriend in five years and was slowly going out of mind from loneliness.

I'm not sure what you mean by deal. —K

We emailed back and forth for weeks, like an old-fashioned courtship, except instead of getting excited about an envelope with a red wax seal, I got excited when I saw his name in my inbox. With every email, it felt more and more like fate. I found out that his business partner lived in *my* building. We must have missed each other by seconds in the lobby. I found out that he went to NYU when I went to NYU. We probably went to the same Halloween party the year I dressed up as Snow White. He lived on Mercer when I lived on Waverly. We probably sat next to each other eating Vegetable Yakisoba at Dojo on West

Fourth. Our lives had been intertwining, intersecting at various points, to bring us to this moment. Imagining all the times we could have met and didn't, all the ways we could have missed each other this time around and didn't, sent chills up my spine. What if I had run down the stairs a minute later? What if that person hadn't farted? What if the train had stopped at my stop?

After about a month of back-and-forth emails I asked him if he wanted to go for a walk in Central Park. If this was the man I was going to spend the rest of my life with, as Harry in *When Harry Met Sally* said, "You want the rest of your life to start as soon as possible."

It was late May, sunny, but still cool. I put on a tight, lightweight gray sweater and a long, gray A-line skirt. I blew my hair out straight and sprayed Clinique's Happy perfume behind my ears. I had just gotten a puppy, a psycho-demon dog my friends called Cujo. I thought about bringing her along on the date, but I was afraid she would bark the entire time and bite him, so I left her at home.

As I approached the Seventy-second Street entrance to the park, I saw Daniel walking toward me. He was wearing his Burberry coat, a navy blue cardigan sweater, slacks and newly polished black leather loafers. I clasped my hands together tight.

"Hi," he said, leaning over and kissing me on the cheek, as if we had already been married for twenty years and it was my turn to say, "How was your day, honey?"

He placed his hand on my lower back and led me to his favorite spot in the park, the bocce ball court, right above

Sheep Meadow. I had walked past it a million times and never noticed it. Standing on my tiptoes, my fingers gripping the chain-link fence, peering at the immaculate field of budding grass, I thought, *This thing, this lawn, has been here all along, just like him.*

We continued to walk along the paths, weaving in and out of trees and strollers and old ladies with canes, stopping by the lake to watch couples kissing in boats.

"I once went on a date with a guy who made me row the boat," I said. I wanted to make sure he wasn't the type to hand me the oars.

"That's lame," he said.

Good answer.

We passed a vending cart. He bought me a bottle of water. We sat down on the grass near the Metropolitan Museum. I noticed a few crumpled leaves stuck to the back of his wool sweater and started to pick them off. He winced, so I stopped.

"This was my father's sweater."

"It's a nice sweater," I said.

"My father died when I was in college."

"I'm so sorry."

He got quiet after that and walked me back to Seventy-second Street.

Fuck. I messed up. Fairytale over.

I was convinced I'd never see him again because I had called attention to his dead father's sweater, but he called me later that night. When I heard his voice, I jumped up and down.

"Hi. I was . . . I was worri . . . how are you?" I asked, not wanting to stick my foot in my mouth again.

"I need you to know something," he said.

Please don't tell me you have AIDS.

"I'm in love with someone else. I'm sorry I didn't tell you today," he said.

Oh God, not again.

"I still want to see you, but it can't get serious," he said.

I knew I should have hung up the phone and told him to never contact me again, but when he asked me if I'd meet him the following day for coffee, I said yes, like a big, fat masochist.

My heart couldn't handle another Zach situation.

As I sipped my latte and listened to Daniel tell me all about Juliette, I felt trapped in a time warp. Another boy. Another girl. Another love just out of reach.

Juliette lived in Paris. *Of course she did.* Daniel's brother-in-law was French and had introduced them several years ago. *How romantic.* Daniel developed a huge crush on her, but Juliette had a boyfriend and he had a girlfriend, and then recently, as in three-months-ago recently, he broke up with his girlfriend and she broke up with her boyfriend and they kissed. "A kiss that changed the world," he said. *Gross.*

I imagined that we were actors in a movie and that this was my cue to throw water in his face. But I didn't have water. All I had was leftover milk foam in my cup. I smiled and tried to act as if I didn't care, that hearing about her didn't hurt me, that I didn't want him to reach over and gently touch my face.

"I wanted you to know my deal," Daniel said.

"Thanks for letting me know," I said.

"Yeah, I had to," he said, shaking his head, as if there were no other option. "I'd still like to hang out with you."

No. No. No.

"Well, I guess we can hang out, but I'm not going to sleep with you."

"Okay. That's fair."

Walk away. Walk away now.

Daniel and I spent every day together for the next month. We took long walks in the park. We went to movies. We ate burritos. We kissed. He even came with me to doggie training school and sat by my side as I fed Cujo raw hot dogs with the hope that she would learn how to sit.

Then he dropped the bomb.

"I'm leaving for Paris next week to see Juliette."

"You what?" I asked.

"I paid for the ticket before I met you."

I felt sucker-punched, the wind knocked out of me, unable to respond.

"I don't know what to do, Kimberlee. I wasn't expecting to like you so much. I usually like thinner girls."

You did not just say that to me.

"More European," he corrected himself. "I really don't know what to do," he added, looking to me for permission.

"Well, if you go to Paris, you'll never see me again," I said, surprising myself with my strength.

The following morning, the phone rang at 7:30 A.M. I didn't have to be at work until 10 A.M. Someone must have died. There must have been another school shooting.

"Hello?" I asked, trying to sound professional.

"I'm not going," Daniel said. "I told Juliette that I met you and that I'm falling in love with you."

I was still half asleep, but it registered.

He chose me. Over her.

I sat up in bed.

"Aren't you happy?" he asked.

"Yes," I said, not quite happy. I wasn't sure what I was.

"I'll pick you up after work," he said, and got off the phone.

I rubbed my eyes.

What just happened? Do I have a boyfriend?

All day at work, I felt both giddy and unsettled. It was another slow news day. I had eight hours to kill, so I signed on to Hotmail, reread every email Daniel had ever sent me, turned on VH1, stared at the clock, made a few phone calls, ordered a Caesar salad with chicken, booked a couple of fiber feeds and waited. Six P.M. finally arrived. I logged off my computer, took the escalator upstairs to the lobby and stepped through the revolving doors onto the street. My life was about to change. I could feel it.

Daniel was standing in front of his blue jeep, illegally parked on Sixth Avenue, holding purple roses. *Purple roses? Strange choice.* I didn't even know there were purple roses.

His hug and kiss felt different. More official. We hopped

in his car and bounced all the way to Hoboken, where he lived, Fatboy Slim's "Praise You" blasting.

When we got to his apartment, he took my hand and led me to his bedroom, past his roommate, a strange older woman who mumbled "hello." He shut the door. I wondered if he thought we were going to have sex. I wasn't ready for that.

He walked over to the wall behind his bed and took down a poster-sized picture of Juliette. *Did he bring me all the way here for this?* I immediately thought about Maggie and the picture of her on Zach's desk. Juliette was no Maggie. That was for sure. She had black curly hair and a big nose. I wondered whether I would have felt more victorious if she had been prettier.

Two months later, Daniel moved in with me.

My studio apartment was only three hundred square feet. There wasn't enough room for both of us and a screaming lunatic dog, so I found Cujo a home in Upstate New York where she could bark and be her crazy self.

I went from taking care of a dog to taking care of a man whose bark *and bite* I would soon learn were much worse.

★ ★ ★

"I was at work on September 11 when the first plane flew into the first Tower," I say to Iris. "My coworker Lisa and I were eating toasted bagels with peanut butter. Karen was working a later shift that day. The newsroom was quiet because from eight to nine everyone is in the morning meeting. Someone pointed to one of the monitors above our heads and screamed. We looked up and saw the first Tower smoking. Everyone in the morning meeting ran out of the war room. As you can imagine, it was pandemonium. We dispatched crews and trucks as we watched WNYW's helicopter shot in horror, and then someone screamed, 'Another one just hit.' People were freaking out and crying. I was calm. For the rest of the day I was tied to the one phone line connected to the field, walking the crew through live shots for the channel and all the affiliates. At one point, I was watching the monitor next to me, when all of a sudden the camera guy dropped the camera to the ground. I didn't know what was going on. All I could see was running feet. Then the shot went black. I thought we had lost transmission but as the smoke and debris dispersed, the scene slowly came back into view. It was terrifying."

"Sounds like a horror film," Iris says. "I was in the Berkshires visiting my daughter and her family at the time. We watched it on television."

"You have a daughter?! Wait. You watch television?" I ask, shocked by both pieces of information.

"Yes, I have a daughter. And grandchildren."

I have a flash of Iris jumping up, running to the kitchen and coming back with framed pictures, but she stays seated.

"I don't usually watch television. As you may have noticed, I don't own a set. But my daughter does, so we watched the coverage. Who didn't that day? That must have been very hard on you."

"I was actually okay," I say. "I think because I grew up with a sick brother, I got used to DEFCON 1."

"Excuse me?"

"You know the red and orange warning levels? It felt like we were always in the red. At a moment's notice, we had to switch into high gear. I'm good at that. But watching people jump out of windows, footage that never aired, that stuff really screws with you."

"I can't imagine."

"I was lucky, though. I know that. Lucky I didn't have to see it in person. Lucky I didn't die. Lucky I didn't know anyone who died. It was a total wake-up call though, like, wow, I *could* die, and the thing was I already felt dead. I know that sounds dramatic, but I hated my life. Things had gotten really bad with Daniel, my boyfriend at the—"

Iris cuts me off. "That was the beauty of September 11. That's the beauty of the Tower card. From the rubble, we have the chance to start over and find a new, more honest way of being."

★   ★   ★

Climbing the subway stairs, I was dreading going home; I never knew what to expect.

I opened the door to find Daniel punching the side of his computer monitor, screaming, "Goddamn fucking Microsoft. I'm going to kill Bill Gates."

I wanted to lock myself in the next room, but there wasn't a next room, and I was tired of sitting in a cold bathtub, trying to ignore his rants about how the world was conspiring against him and how he didn't understand why all the venture capitalists he met wouldn't give him a mere $500,000. He kept telling me I was the only one who understood his creative genius, and I kept thinking, *If I buy*

185

him sneakers, if I cook him dinner, if I make his life easy, then he'll be able to love me in the way I need to be loved.

"My life is shit," he screamed.

"Daniel," I said, stepping toward him slowly, "maybe you should get a regular job. I mean, you seem unhappy and I could use some help with the bills."

"Give me a fucking break!" he spat. "You sound like my fucking mother!"

I wanted to scream, "Get over your shit with your mother and father and grow the fuck up already." But before I had the chance to respond, Daniel lunged out of his chair, threw me onto the floor and held my arms down. "Can't you see how hard I work?" he yelled, his mouth contorting, his face turning red.

"Get off me," I squeezed out with what little air I had left and managed to kick him in the side.

"Don't you know I'm working my ass off?" he asked, his nose touching mine.

"Get off me!"

When had my life become a bad Lifetime movie?

"Fine," he spat, and stormed out of the apartment, mumbling, "Fuck this shit."

I rolled onto my side and raised my body up on wobbly arms. I stepped into the bathroom, put both hands on the rim of the sink and stared at my face in the mirror. My eyes looked dead, black, opaque. I didn't recognize myself. I washed my face, blew my nose and crawled into bed with my work clothes still on. I had no idea where Daniel had gone, but when he got back, I was asleep.

I started to sleep a lot.

Every day when I came home from work, I took a nap. At first it was one hour, then two, then three, then before long, I was sleeping through to the next morning. Daniel sometimes tried to wake me up for dinner or a walk in the park, but I could barely open my eyes.

My mother was beginning to worry. She didn't know about Daniel's temper or the fact that our fights got so bad the neighbors would complain. She just didn't like that I was sleeping my life away.

"Kimmi, maybe something is wrong. Maybe you should see a doctor."

I made an appointment to see an acupuncturist who told me I was Yin-deficient and that my Chi wasn't flowing properly. *No duh.* Then I saw a holistic health counselor who told me to eat quinoa and kale. *Fuck that!* I was not about to give up ice cream! Finally, I went to a real doctor, Dr. Grostein, a small, bald, seventy-year-old hematologist who ran every blood test known to man to rule out lupus, chronic fatigue syndrome, Lyme disease and God knows what else.

Sitting in a paper gown on the edge of a cold table, I waited for him to come in and tell me my test results.

The door swung open.

"Nothing's wrong with you," he said. "On paper, you're as strong as a horse."

"I don't feel so strong," I said, wanting to curl up in a ball. "I sleep all the time. My hair is falling out. I have this weird rash on my face."

"Get on the scale."

"What?"

"Get on the scale."

I climbed off of the table and let him weigh me.

Holy shit.

I had gained twenty pounds.

"You're fat. You need to lose weight. You could start with that."

How did that happen?

"I guess sleep and ice cream are my only real comforts," I admitted, ashamed of what I had become.

"What else is going on in your life?" he asked.

"Well, my boyfriend. He doesn't have a job. And, well, sometimes our fights get violent."

Whoa, I said it aloud.

Not one muscle moved on his face. He didn't seem surprised or alarmed.

"You know what you need to do then. And lose that weight too," he said, patting me on the knee before he left the room.

That's it? No psychiatrist referral? No intervention hotline? No Prozac?

I called my mother and told her nothing was wrong with me, that the blood tests had come back normal.

"I'm taking you out to dinner tonight," she said, in a firm, parental voice I wasn't used to hearing from her. I didn't have the strength to say no, so I met her at Sarabeth's Kitchen on Columbus and Eightieth Street.

She wrapped her arms around me like the mama bear I

remembered from childhood. My body felt limp, my arms were dangling at my sides. I wanted her to take me home with her, cook me soup, give me a hot water bottle. I wished she lived in a house in the country, so I could really get away.

"Mom, he said nothing was wrong," I cried.

"I know, Kimmi, I know."

We sat down at a corner table and ordered their soup and salad special.

"He said I was fat."

"You're not fat."

"Yes, I am," I said, lowering my shoulders, wiping tears from my eyes.

"Kimmi, you know. You can always make different choices. It's never too late. I did it. I got out. You can too."

"Mom, I have a hard time getting out of bed in the morning."

She held my hand. "I know, sweetie. I know."

Later that night, my father called, his voice sharp and urgent. "You live in a dinky apartment. You sleep your life away. You're in a job you don't like. You're with a man who doesn't have a job. You don't have money to go out and do things. My heart breaks for your life."

I pulled the covers over my head and said, "It's my life, Dad. I'll figure it out." Who was I fooling? I barely had the energy to change my underwear, let alone change my life.

A few days later, American Airlines Flight 11 crashed into the North Tower of the World Trade Center.

I heard a voice inside me shout, "MOVE OVER. NEW

MANAGEMENT IS IN DA HOOOUUSE!" Apparently this was my higher self. I wasn't sure why she sounded like a big black woman named Malvina or where she had been hiding, but there she was, as clear as a bright blue sky, screaming at me to wake up. "You are the one, child, the only one, who can save yourself! Never let a man walk all over you. Never!"

Everything that happened from that moment on felt surreal, out of body, as if I were a wooden marionette and Malvina was controlling my every move. She was the strength and energy I had been waiting for, pulling my ass out of bed and setting me into motion again. "There'll be plenty of time to sleep when you're dead. Right now, you gotta start living your damn life."

She didn't think "fat" was my problem, but she threw out my Ben & Jerry's Mint Chocolate Cookie ice cream anyway, telling me, "Even the skinniest person on the planet shouldn't be living on this shit." She stocked the fridge with fruits and vegetables, and found me a therapist with a PhD. Something was wrong with my head, and she was not going to stand by and let me fade into oblivion. Not on her watch. Then she did the unthinkable. She told Daniel he had until December 1 to get a job or get out.

This woman inside me was incredible. Everything she said she was going to do, she did. Everything she wanted, she got.

When December 1 rolled around, and Daniel still didn't have a job, she packed up his stuff and took back his keys. "Listen, we'll still date. You just have to get a job and learn to become more independent," she said, lying through *my* teeth. Then she drove his ass all the way down to South Carolina to stay with his sister. "Pass the baton, baby girl!"

With Daniel seven hundred miles away, it was much easier to tell him the truth.

"Listen Daniel, I don't love you anymore."

"But what if I get a job?"

"It's too late."

"What if I go down on you more? I know I didn't do that that much and I'm sorry," he said, thinking oral sex would be the key to my heart.

"It's over," I said, and hung up the phone, feeling like a balloon being released into the open sky.

Done and done!

But Malvina wasn't done with me.

She moved me into a spacious one-bedroom apartment in the same building; she painted my living room cranapple-red; she feng shui'd my furniture; and she saged each room. "If you ever need me again, I'm right here," she said, and patted my chest.

Sitting on my couch in my new living room, I couldn't believe this was my life—no one screaming at Bill Gates, no one punching the computer, no one hurting me.

THE SUN.

El Sol / Le Soleil
Arcana: XVIIII
Path on Kabbalah Tree of Life: 30
Color: Orange
Planet: Sun
Constellation: The Twins
Musical note: D

chapter nine
the sun

"Sunlight and singing welcome your coming."
—E. E. Cummings

"Here comes the sun and I say it's all right," Iris sings, and then says, "Now, wasn't that worth it?"

"Worth what?" I ask.

"I knew all along it was going to get better," she says, handing me the Sun card.

"What are you talking about?"

"You shuffled the cards. I placed them in the spread. I saw the map. I didn't know the details. But I knew the cards. And I had an idea of where we were headed."

"So you've been reading my future this whole time?"

"No, I've been reading your life. It's not the same. I knew the cards and their meaning and their placement and I knew the sun would be coming out. I didn't know you had a sick brother. I didn't know what kinds of problems you had with your mother, only that there were some. And I didn't know you had a sexual encounter with a shark," she says, and smiles. "Now tell me what you see."

"I see sunflowers," I say, counting four sunflowers. "An enormous sun with an expressionless face. An orange flag. A naked child on top of a white horse. Wait. There was a white horse in the Death card. This one looks like a baby horse. Does that mean something?"

"A return to innocence," Iris says.

"By Enigma? My mom used to love that song."

"It's a good one. Not as good as 'Here Comes the Sun.'"

"Did I tell you I've woken up to a Muzak version of 'Here Comes the Sun' for the past twenty years? I still have the pink Swatch alarm clock I had in seventh grade."

"That's quite an achievement."

"Yes, I guess it is."

Iris and I shift in our seats at the same time, smiling at each other, eyes locked. For the first time, I think of her as a friend who's just lived a little more life than I have.

"So, the Sun?" I say.

"Yup," she says back.

"What does it mean?"

"I thought you'd never ask," she says, and lifts her arms toward the ceiling. "The Sun comes at the point in the

Fool's journey when he thinks it can't get worse. He's gone through the dark night of the soul and finally emerges in daylight."

"That's what I felt like when I broke up with Daniel, like I was seeing daylight for the first time in a long time."

★ ★ ★

I was leaning against a candlelit bar at my friend Jaime's thirtieth birthday party, ordering a sidecar with Hennessy and sugar on the rim. Jaime was the first of my high school friends to turn thirty. She had been dreading thirty, studying the new wrinkles under her eyes, plucking the lonesome gray hairs out of her head, waiting for her ass to drop. I was looking forward to thirty. I felt as though I had earned my age.

"Wow. You look great," Stephanie, one of Jaime's college friends, said. She looked me up and down and turned to her boyfriend. "Doesn't she look great?"

I had lost ten pounds. My hair was long and wavy and my cheeks glowed.

"Yeah, she looks great," her boyfriend said. "Hey, I heard you broke up with Daniel. Good call on that one. He was a dick."

These were people who barely knew me, barely knew Daniel, and they knew he was bad for me. It was as if I had been walking around New York City with toilet paper stuck to my shoe. Everyone could see it, except me. The more parties I went to, the more people I saw, the more I learned how everyone hated Daniel and had wanted us to break up. My best friend Mari's *cousin* admitted to calling him "trench coat Mafia" behind his back. The Burberry coat I had thought was old-fashioned and charming, others found plain creepy.

Maybe if more people had said something sooner, I wouldn't have missed all those hours of sunlight. Then again, there had been someone in my life who wasn't afraid to tell it to me straight: my father. I just never listened.

The first Mark Auerbach "sit-down" happened over spareribs and fried rice.

"Kimma, Zach doesn't comb his hair. What self-respecting man doesn't comb his hair?" my father asked, barbecue sauce smeared all over his chin.

"Dad, I like Zach's wild, curly hair."

He refused to buy into the sex appeal of bed-head.

"He doesn't look me in the eye either. Big red flag, in my book," he said.

I ate my fortune cookie, thanked him for dinner and continued to date Zach for another two years.

The Daniel "sit-down" was different. It happened over $30 Veal Milanese. My father was back on top and could afford SoHo Italian again.

My father liked Daniel. That wasn't the problem. He had given him suits and ties and put him in touch with venture capitalists. He had tried everything in his power to ensure that his "future son-in-law" would be positioned properly to take care of his baby girl. But once he saw that Daniel's company wasn't taking off and I was still paying all the bills, he insisted Daniel develop a "plan B." When Daniel refused his advice, my father turned to me.

"I don't want you to enable him," my father said, taking a sip of his wine. "If I keep giving you money and you keep taking care of him, then he will never feel the pressure to get a real job."

At that point, things were good between Daniel and me. I still believed in him.

"Dad, I don't know how to say this, but I'm used to you expressing your love for me with money. If you're not going to help me financially, you're going to have to figure out another way to love me."

He paused, pulled out his checkbook and wrote me a check for $500. "I'll try to give you more hugs," he said, and patted me on the back with one hand.

Whoever I dated next, I wanted to avoid another "sitdown" with my father.

I wasn't sure I was ready to date again anyway. I wanted to eat well, work out, see friends, and take care of myself. I was enjoying my new apartment, my new body, my new life. And I had just discovered a new favorite pastime: Google. I loved to Google everything and everyone. It was safe and fun and kept me occupied for hours.

Sometime in early February, I was sitting at work, bored out of my mind, looking up old friends. I typed "Jonathon Block" into the search bar. I knew Jonathon from SUNY Purchase. He worked in the film department and had patiently taught me how to edit my first documentary video. My friend Clover thought we were perfectly matched. I was a Rat, he was a Dragon, and according to her books, Rats and Dragons got along great. When Jonathon invited me to his wedding, I knew the stars were not aligned for us. It had been seven years since I had seen or spoken to Jonathon. I wondered what he was doing, how life was treating him, so I emailed him. He emailed me back and told me he was separated from his wife, he had a three-year-old son and he thought of me often.

Thought of me often.

I wasn't sure why that touched me the way it did. I had moved around so much, I had met so many people, been so many places. Sometimes I didn't feel attached to time or place, as if my experiences existed only in bubbles in my mind. The fact that this kind man from so long ago re-membered me and "thought of me often" made me feel real, that I mattered.

We met at Pershing Square, a restaurant directly across the street from Grand Central Station, on Valentine's Day. He handed me a pink rose and gave me a bear hug. He looked good, the same. He was slightly balding then and he was slightly balding now. We sat down in a booth by a win-dow. I ordered chicken. He ordered fish. We barely touched our food. We were too busy talking about our failed rela-tionships. When the check came, he paid for dinner.

"Thank you so much!" I said, as if he had just given me a gold necklace.

"Really, it's no big deal."

"I haven't had someone be this nice to me in a long time."

"You're easy to be nice to," he said, squeezing my hand.

He called me a car service and kissed me good night. I

told him I wanted to take it slow, especially after what I had just been through with Daniel. He said that was fine. He was going through a lot too.

"When can I meet your son?" I asked him a couple weeks later, forgetting we had agreed to take it slow.

"One day," he said.

But "one day" didn't seem to be coming. He spent every weekend with his son, and I could never get through to him after 7 P.M., which made me wonder if things weren't as over with his wife as I thought they were.

"Jonathon, I know I said I didn't want to move too fast, but I want to meet your son. I want to be able to spend weekends with you."

"Kimberlee, my life is complicated. My son is my priority right now. I really don't think I can give you the attention you need and deserve."

So I ended it. Just like that. I didn't linger for two years. I didn't crawl back into bed, wishing he could love me the way I needed to be loved. I made a choice, bold and strong, and felt Malvina with me.

Still, I cried. I knew I would rather spend the rest of my life alone than be with some jackass freeloader or a man who was only maybe separated from his wife. I just needed some reassurance that my life wasn't going to be a series of mistakes, so I called my best friend Mari and begged her to meet me for coffee.

It was a rainy day in late March. My eyes were still puffy from crying.

"Kimmi, you have to think about yourself," Mari said,

handing me her napkin. "Stop putting so much energy into men and put some energy into you."

"I know," I said, blowing my nose. "They say 'when you're happy and least expecting it, that's when you find true love.' But what if I'm not a happy person? What if I'm just prone to depression?"

Mari leaned forward, and in a low voice, whispered, "You *have* to get out of Sad Kimmiland." Mari and I had known each other since high school. She knew when I was spiraling into my dark place.

"It's not so much Jonathon that's making me sad. It's the hope. I felt hope with him, and now it's gone."

"You do realize how pathetic you're being?" Mari asked, and started laughing.

"Yeah," I said, and smiled.

"At least you don't have that awful acne you had in college. Remember that?"

"Yeah, I remember that."

"And you came to visit me in Vermont and I tried to put makeup on you, but it was pointless. Your face was just covered in pimples.

"That was so gross," I said, laughing.

The waitress came over to ask us if we wanted refills.

"What time is it?" I asked.

"Six fifteen."

"No, thanks, just the check," I said and turned to Mari. "There's a Moth StorySLAM tonight. The theme is music and I was thinking about telling my Adam Duritz story."

Mari was a comedian. I had watched her perform at countless open mics over the years.

"That's awesome. That's exactly what I'm talking about. I have to be on the Upper East Side in an hour. Shit. I wish I could go with you!"

We walked in the rain over to the Nuyorican Poets Cafe on East Third Street. Mari hugged me good-bye, our umbrellas bumping and twisting together, and said, "You're going to kill." I knew she meant well, but storytelling wasn't about "killing." In comedy, you make people laugh or you die. Kill or be killed. With storytelling, the point is to connect with people and take them on a journey.

Waiting in line, I listened to the people in front of me talk about following monkeys in Costa Rica. I wanted to tell them about my trip to Costa Rica, but I was too nervous to open my mouth and wanted to save my energy for my story. I had never been to a Moth StorySLAM before. I used to volunteer for their professional storytelling shows before Daniel and I met, before I went into hiding. The Moth had grown and now had three branches: professional storytelling shows, an outreach program and StorySLAMs.

They opened the doors. The line started to move up. I paid my five bucks and found a folding chair toward the back. I put my jacket down and walked to the stage to see how to sign up.

"Write your name on a piece of paper and stick it in the hat," Jenifer Hixson, the MothSLAM producer, instructed me. I complimented her on her cowboy boots as

I wrote down my name, email address and phone number on a little piece of paper. I folded it and prayed. *Please pick me.* Then I placed it gently inside the enormous, sequined sombrero and walked back to my seat.

The room filled up fast. Soon there were no more seats left. People were standing by the bar. Some had made their way up to the balcony. And others were standing directly behind me. This was turning out to be a packed house, close to two hundred people.

Can I really do this? In front of all these people?

At 7:15 P.M., the house lights dimmed and comedian Shelagh Ratner, the host, stood at the mic. "Sorry I'm late. I was watching the Oscars and Halle Berry was *still* talking." When people didn't laugh, she went on to make fun of Greta Van Susteren's new face. I winced. I didn't want to think about Fox. Not now. Not here. "Come back to me, people," she said. "It's just you and me all night." Everyone laughed. The room was hers. "Okay, for those of you who haven't been to a MothSLAM before, let me explain. Tonight's theme is music. We're going to pick ten names out of the hat. Each storyteller gets five minutes to tell a story with a beginning, middle and end. If someone goes over time, the lovely Jen Hixon will blow a whistle. Are you all ready?" she said, and proceeded to pick the first name.

It wasn't mine.

A man in a blue sweater stepped in front of the mic and told a story about catering a gay party and stripping to a Prince song for $900. People laughed. People clapped.

The judges held up their scorecards. "7.0" "8.0" "7.0" The crowd booed. He smiled and picked the next name out of the hat.

Again, not mine. This was torture. My knees were bouncing. My palms were sweating. I wanted them to call my name already.

The next storyteller was an old, blind man wearing a nylon windbreaker. His dark glasses covered most of his face and his silver hair stuck out from under his Boston Red Sox baseball cap. He told a story about his Japanese wife and how they fell in love. Then he sang George Gershwin's "For You, For Me, For Evermore," his voice shaking with emotion. The crowd clapped wildly. "9.0" "8.8" "8.4" They placed the sombrero in his hands so he could feel around for the next storyteller.

Please don't let it be me. I can't follow a blind man.

"Kimmi?"

Shit!

"Kimmi Auerbach?"

That was my name, but only my parents and closest friends called me Kimmi. Why were they calling me "Kimmi?" Oh right, because my email was on the little piece of paper I had stuck inside the hat.

"Kimmi?"

I walked through the crowd and stepped on stage. The lights were beating down on me. Every eye in the room was looking at *me*. I took a deep breath and started my story with, "Okay, so I was living with my parents in Connecticut in 1994. I had cut my hair really short. I had gone off the Pill. I had severe acne. I was very unattractive. I had just broken up with my boyfriend of three years. I was very depressed and upset and fell in love with Adam Duritz of the Counting Crows."

The crowd laughed.

I proceeded to tell my young-girl-in-love-with-a-rock-star story, how I made Adam a silk painting, bought him a book, met him at The Beacon Theater and ended up getting into a fight with him about art at his New York City wrap party at the Iridium.

The whistle blew. I had gone over time, but it was okay. My story was almost over.

"I leave the party and start crying. I get into a cab. The cab driver says, 'Are you OK, sweetie?' 'I really don't know. And I don't think I have money to tip you.'"

Everyone laughed.

"'It's OK, sweetie.' He turns off the meter and I think, 'Here's this guy, this nameless guy, who has so much more soul than the person I had put so much stock in.'"

People clapped, hollered and hooted.

I did it!

I told my story in front of two hundred strangers. I hadn't written it down. I hadn't practiced. I just spoke from my heart. And I made people care.

I waited on stage for my score.

"9.3" "9.2" 9.2"

Holy shit! I could win.

I picked the next name out of the hat and made my way back through the crowd.

"You were great."

"Yeah, that was awesome."

"I loved your story."

I felt like a movie star and blushed. I wasn't used to this kind of attention.

For the rest of the night, I sat and listened to other people's stories and felt part of something bigger. I loved the Moth. I loved these people. I loved this feeling.

The last storyteller got up onstage. I still had the highest score. I wanted him to do well—just not better than me. And he didn't.

The host tallied up the scores.

"Kimmi is the winner! Get up here, Kimmi. Come get your prize."

The prize was a standing ovation. I bowed and giggled and held my hands to my heart in gratitude. I thought I might cry. I had never done Ecstasy, but I imagined it must feel similar to this wild pulsing through my body. I never could have felt this way with Daniel *or* Jonathon. No man could ever give me this feeling. Mari was right. This feeling came from within me. This was all me. On my way home, I left a message for her, telling her I had officially left Sad Kimmiland. As long as I had a story to tell, I had a feeling I wouldn't be returning.

A few months later, Mari suggested I try JDate. "I think you're ready, Kimmi. You're much happier than you've ever been. You know what you want and what you don't want. This is the perfect way to be intentional while letting fate take its course. You'll love it."

On July 17, 2002, I posted my profile on JDate:

More about me: *I am passionate and full of life. I love to laugh, and when I laugh, I laugh loud and hard. I am a great listener and love to ask people questions.*

This is what I've learned from my past: *I have learned that you can't change people and that you should never fall in love with someone's potential.*

Three days later, I got an email:

Dear Kimberlee,
 Congratulations! A member of the JDate.com network would like to contact you!

234778 wrote:
"Hi, I'm Noah. You sound great."

I was five minutes early, sitting on a plush leather couch in the Hudson Hotel, on Fifty-eighth and Eighth. I had just come from therapy and was feeling a little raw. Maybe it wasn't such a good idea to set up a blind date after therapy. It was too late. He was already on his way.

I had set up dates with five different guys in one week. I had already been out with an entertainment lawyer who lied about his height and an unemployed stockbroker who lied about his age. Noah was date number three. Out of all of them, he was the only one I hadn't contacted first.

Most of the men who reached out to me were twenty years older, looking for arm candy. I had no desire to be that again.

I was wearing red lipstick, a black pencil skirt, a white button-down shirt and a turquoise and coral necklace I had made myself. I had seen two pictures of Noah online, one color and one black and white. In the color one, he was smiling and had longish reddish hair. In the black-and-white shot, he had short hair and looked kind of conservative. I didn't know who I'd get, Shaggy or Fred. Playing with the hem of my skirt, I spotted him through the glass wall coming up the escalator. *Shaggy. Yes!*

His hair was more ginger than red. He was wearing brown plastic glasses and he had a magazine tucked into the back pocket of his jeans. Everything about him was casual and reminded me of the beach. I watched him enter the lobby. He stopped to admire the outdoor garden behind the concierge desk. There was a stillness about him. Looking at him was like staring out at the ocean. I felt my entire body relax.

He turned around and our eyes met. Smiles flashed across our faces, as if we were old friends who hadn't seen each other in a long time.

"Hi," I mouthed.

"Hi," he mouthed back.

He walked over to me and shook my hand. It was the first time in my life I was less aware of the handshake and more aware of the eye contact. He looked into me, straight to my soul.

I ordered a sidecar. He ordered a martini. We dove right in.

"I'm glad I'm meeting you," he said, shaking his head. "I was done with JDate. It wasn't working out for me. You're my last date."

"That's funny. You're my third date," I said. "I just signed up."

We marveled at our luck and continued to talk about work and therapy and sex.

"I once kissed a girl," I admitted, not sure if I was confessing or trying to turn him on. I laughed and spilled some Hennessy onto my leg, which, I later found out, turned him on more than my girl-on-girl kiss and that he had had the urge to lick it off.

He told me he worked as a technology consultant, but was a songwriter and was developing several art and theater projects too. I told him that I also had a technical job but wanted to be a storyteller and writer. We then moved on to our childhoods and discovered we both had sick brothers. His brother didn't get sick until later in life, so it was different. But still, it created an instant bond between us. We both knew what it was like to be the "healthy" one, to spring into action, to put our own needs aside.

When he got up to go to the bathroom, I wrote down the name of two books I thought he'd like on the side of a Hudson Hotel matchbox. On the other side, I wrote: "You are lovely." I didn't think he'd notice it until he got home, but when I handed it to him, it was the first thing he saw.

"You are too," he said, and smiled.

We both had dinner plans with other people, so after two hours, he paid the check and we walked to the corner and hugged good-bye. I had the strangest feeling, something I had never felt before. Even if I never saw him again, I was happy to have met someone I liked, which meant I *knew* what I liked. I waited for him to turn the corner and called my mother.

"Mom, I met the nicest man. He was sweet and cute. Gentle. Smart. Super smart." I went on and on, bouncing down the street, smiling so big my cheeks hurt.

"Kimmi, I've never heard you talk about a man like this before," she said.

"I know. I know," I said. "I'll be over in a few minutes."

"What would you like for dinner?" she asked.

"Same old?" I asked back.

We couldn't get enough of Miss Elle's lemon chicken.

When I walked through the door of my mother's apartment, she gave me a big hug, stepped back and said, "You're glowing. You're absolutely glowing."

As I stretched out on the couch in her living room, she grabbed her camera and snapped a shot.

"Why did you do that?" I asked, blinking from the flash.

"Because I have a feeling today is a special day. That you have met your person."

"Maybe," I mused.

Noah emailed me later that night:

From: Noah G.
To: kimberleedawn
Subject: Tonight

Kimberlee,
I just got in. How was dinner with your mom? I had a
great time with you tonight. I'd like to see you again.
Noah

I wanted him to see me again. I had never been so seen before.

★   ★   ★

"The rays of the Sun show the Fool his own light," Iris says. "This card is coming up in your other person position, which means you have met someone who shows you your light."

"I definitely feel like Noah shows me my light. He did from the second I met him. After our first date, I didn't bother going out with anyone else. I canceled my other dates and my JDate accou—"

"JDate?" Iris asks, not getting the reference.

"Online dating for Jews. You can choose the level of Jew you want. High-Holy-Day Jew. Orthodox Jew. Secular Jew. Never goes to temple but dresses well and likes to eat bagels on the weekend Jew. My best friend Mari met her husband on JDate. He clicked kosher. She didn't. But now she keeps a kosher home."

"Are you happy with Noah?" Iris asks me.

"People have asked me all sorts of questions about

Noah. Why doesn't he want to get married? How long are you going to wait? Does he want kids? But never a simple 'Are you happy?' Yes. I am happy. It's easy to forget that. There's so much pressure to get to the next level."

"Sometimes we're not meant to get to the next level with the person we're with."

"Are you saying Noah and I aren't meant to be together?" I ask, afraid she knows something I don't.

"I knew you were going to think that. No, I'm saying that we can learn something about ourselves from each person who comes into our lives. Sometimes we're meant to learn a particular lesson and move on. Sometimes we find a person who helps us grow over a lifetime. There are people who meet in high school and stay together their whole lives—although that is becoming more and more rare—and others who have many deep relationships."

"Like my father, who is on his fourth marriage?"

"Come on, Kimberlee. No judgment here. That's the thing you have to realize. There is no right way to do this. That's what trips people up. They think their life should look a certain way, their relationship should be like this or like that. It's misguided. We're all here on this earth trying to move forward, trying to learn from our mistakes, trying to find meaning."

"Do you believe in marriage?" I ask.

"Yes. Most certainly. I was married for thirty-three glorious years to the biggest pain in the ass on the planet and I loved every minute of it. I miss him. Do I need to get married again? No. Did I learn all my lessons? No. But that's okay. There will be other people. Who knows? You might even teach me something," she says, and smiles. "One of the beauties of marriage is the opportunity for long-term mirroring, and by that, I mean having the opportunity to look at yourself and understand who you really are in a deep way. Have you ever read Martin Buber?"

I shake my head "no."

"Well, I love how he put it. He believes that the problem with romantic love is that it's based on a feeling and when that feeling goes away, people often look for it with someone else, but then that feeling goes away, and you're forever chasing a feeling. Some might find that fun, but I like the depth you get from love's ebb and flow, something a good marriage or long-term relationship affords us. When we are mirrored and challenged and loved over a lifetime, our potential is endless. We can go as deep as the sea. Buber didn't say the part about the sea. That's all me," Iris says, and winks, her eyes now as bright as the bluest sapphires.

"I like that. I think a lot about why I want to get married so badly. Is it because all my friends are married? Is it because it's what you do? Is it because society accepts you more if you're married? I look at all these women in the gym, on the subway, at work, and I stare at the diamonds on their fingers, and think, 'Someone chose them. They're worth something.'"

"Kimberlee, a diamond does not define worth. Not real worth, anyway. If you spend your entire life worrying about being chosen, waiting for someone else to make a decision about you, where does that leave you?"

"I don't think I'm waiting for Noah to make a decision about me. I was. I mean, that's what I was doing. But I think I stopped."

"Good," Iris says. "It's much better to be the subject in your life rather than an object."

"The thing is, I'm happy with Noah. I feel better about myself because of him. But he's not ready for marriage and I am. And because I moved around so much as a kid, I really crave home. A warm, inviting, safe home."

"Why can't you have that?"

"I don't know, Iris. I really don't know. Even our couples therapist thinks we have a great relationship. He says he sees couples all the time, married, unmarried, who don't have half the love we have."

"Well, love is not always enough. It's about how well a couple can negotiate a life together. First of all, can they agree on a life? And then, can they build it together without killing each other?" she says, and laughs. "Seriously, those are questions you have to ask yourself. You, and only you, can answer them. If you think about your reading so far, this struggle makes a lot of sense. You haven't trusted yourself in the past and that makes these kinds of decisions all the more difficult."

★   ★   ★

Noah and I sat in a circle with eight other couples listening to Roberta Flack's song "The First Time Ever I Saw Your Face." We were at a two-day couples' workshop in Upstate New York. There were boxes of tissues scattered across the carpet. People were sitting on beanbags. Some were leaning against the wall. I was sitting cross-legged, trying not to laugh. It wasn't the song per se. The song was fine. Roberta Flack's voice is hauntingly beautiful. But listening to it with a bunch of strangers, being asked to remember the first time you laid eyes on your "beloved" had to be the cheesiest, most ridiculous, Stuart Smalley bullshit I had ever experienced. I bit my lower lip and tried not to peek at Noah, afraid that if I saw him trying to stifle a laugh too, I would really lose it. I took a deep breath and thought about dead pandas. That's what Mari did every time she tried not to laugh.

Your face . . . Your face . . . Your faaaaaacccccccceeeeeee . . .

The song ended and the facilitator told us to open our eyes.

Thank God for dead pandas.

The woman sitting across from me, who was maybe forty and on the verge of a divorce, was crying. I apologized to her with my eyes, but she probably read it as empathy, not knowing I had been making fun of the exercise in my head.

I turned to Noah, who was trying hard to remain present and open. His sweet brown eyes. His deep smile lines. The dandruff that collected around his temples. I loved this man. What other man would go to a workshop like this with me? What other man would ever love me as much as he loves me? Why were we here again?

For the rest of the weekend, we were asked to find a

corner of the house and "Imago." We weren't sure if anyone else had made Imago a verb, but we liked using it that way. This "Imago" workshop was based on the work of Harville Hendrix. The basic idea is that we attract people into our lives who help us heal from old wounds and that a couple will usually fight over the same three things over and over, and that the only way through it is by listening, validating and empathizing. Noah and I thought we might be able to understand each other better, but the more cookies we ate and the more conversations we had sitting across from each other repeating what the other person had said and empathizing, the more we realized we didn't have that many problems.

Sure, there were things we didn't like about each other. I didn't like that when he felt uncomfortable he would shut down, and he didn't like that when I felt uncomfortable I overcompensated and thought it was my responsibility to make everyone happy and keep the conversation going. But those weren't deal breakers.

I raised my hand.

"I'm confused. Let's say you communicate effectively. You share your feelings. You respect and love each other. Not a problem. But one of you wants to get married and have kids and the other one isn't sure. What then?" I asked, hoping she'd have the perfect answer and that Noah and I would walk out of that post-and-beam house full of sad couples ready to walk down the aisle.

The facilitator, a woman in her late fifties, with curly brown hair and a toned yoga body, pulled her knees to her chest, and said, "You have to make a choice. When I married my husband, he already had two kids, and he made it perfectly clear that he did not want more kids. I was fine with that. His were enough for me. But when I turned forty, everything changed. I wanted kids desperately. I craved them. I couldn't shake it. So we talked about it, and again he made it perfectly clear that he did not want more kids. I had a choice to make. I could have left him and found someone else to have children with. But I stayed, and for two years I mourned. It broke my heart. But I don't regret my decision. He is my choice."

I nodded so she would think she had given me the answer I needed to hear, but she hadn't. I didn't want to have to let go of the idea of marriage and kids. But I also didn't want to break up with Noah.

La Justicia / La Justice
Arcana: VIII
Path on Kabbalah Tree of Life: 22
Color: Green
Astrological sign: Libra
Constellation: The Balance
Musical note: F Sharp

chapter ten

justice

"The fire of Self-knowledge reduces
all Karma to ashes."
—BHAGAVAD GITA

"**Y**ou know it's not your fault, right?"
Iris asks me.

"What's not my fault?"

"Noah's not being ready to get married. It doesn't
mean there's something wrong with you," Iris says as if she
wants to reach over and give me a hug.

"I'm not sure about that," I say. "I was kind of a nightmare in the beginning. Sometimes I think you can't get
over that stuff, that it stays with you forever."

★   ★   ★

Noah and I walked across East Tenth over to Second Avenue. We were going to see two of his friends from college dance at St. Mark's Church.

"And you never dated either of them?" I asked for the third time.

"No, Kimberlee, they're just friends."

It was early February. We had already been together for six months, but we still hadn't said "I love you." I was waiting for him to say it first. It was driving me crazy. I kept thinking about all the ways I could say it. I could write it in steam on his bathroom mirror. I could put it on a yellow Post-it and stick it on a milk carton in his fridge. I could draw it in red lipstick across his chest while he slept.

Why wasn't he saying it?

Noah felt the weight of words in a way I didn't. I often said things I didn't mean. I did things I didn't want to do. I was nice when I felt like being nasty. And I said, "I love you" to just about anyone who warmed my heart.

As we entered the theater, dancers were still scurrying around the stage, trying to get ready for the show. Noah's "friends" spotted us and yelled, "Hey, Noah!"

I stood there, my hands clasped tightly together, while they reached over and gave Noah a tit-sandwich hug.

"It's SO nice to meet you," the one with the curly blond hair said.

"Yes, you too," I said, nodding and smiling a little too much.

"Well, we gotta run," the other one said, and twirled

around. I stared at her ass as she ran away. It was much cuter than mine. I wanted to go home.

"Come on. Lets get seats," Noah said, pulling me up to the top-right bleacher. A big pole blocked my vision, but I didn't care. I didn't need a better view.

The first act was a woman changing hats. She was blantantly ripping off Beckett. The second act was an elaborate number with kicking legs, swinging butts and flying arms. Noah's friends were two of the fourteen and were only onstage for a couple of minutes. The third act was a man and a woman. Their dance was sensual and beautiful and kind of felt like watching porn, their bodies twisting and grinding. I could feel a roll of fat jut out over my tights. The last act of the night was a solo piece: a woman writhing on the floor to the song "I'm Ready," by Tracy Chapman.

Everyone was silent, riveted.

"Isn't she amazing?" Noah whispered.

If you think she's so amazing, why don't you be with her?

When the song ended, the entire audience rose to their feet, applauding louder and more enthusiastically than they had for anyone else.

What does she have that I don't?

I turned to Noah. "What's so special about her?"

"Kimberlee, she doesn't have legs."

I looked back down at the stage. Sure enough, she didn't have legs. I couldn't understand for the life of me how I could have missed something like that. I wanted to crawl under my chair.

I was jealous of a legless woman.

"What's wrong, Kimberlee?" he asked.

"I'm not feeling well. I gotta go." I said, and bolted out of my seat.

Noah ran after me. "Wait, Kimberlee. Let me say good-bye to my friends and I'll go with you."

I waited for him outside, shivering.

Five minutes later, Noah put his hand around my waist and said, "Come on, let's go back to my apartment."

When we got inside, I took off my coat, sat down on his bed, covered my face with my hands and started to cry.

"What's going on, baby?"

"You're not going to like it."

"What?" he asked.

"I'm a very jealous person."

"It's okay," he said, and hugged me.

"No, really," I said.

Noah got up and flipped through his record collection. He pulled one out, slipped it on, placed the needle down and got into bed with me.

Looking for the key to set me free
Oh the jealousy, the greed is the unraveling

I hadn't heard "All I Want" or the sound of a crackling record in years. I felt comforted by her voice, but it was going to take a lot more than a Joni Mitchell song to set me free.

★   ★   ★

"I look back at my life," I say to Iris, "and think about all the mean things I've done, all the ugliness in me, and I can't

222

help but wonder if that's not why Noah isn't ready to get married, if that's not why all these things have happened to me, being cheated on, getting crabs, being in an abusive relationship. It all feels like punishment."

"You and punishment," Iris says, and shakes her head. "We're not talking about breaking the law here. In matters of the heart, we punish ourselves. If you don't learn how to forgive yourself and move on, you'll forever be trapped in the past," Iris says, and hands me the next card. "This is what you fear *but want* most."

"Justice?" I ask.

The woman pictured in the card is holding a sword in her right hand and a balance scale in her left. There's something regal about her, the way she's sitting, her deep red and gold robe. She looks as if she's judging me.

"Justice is about righting the wrongs of our past. Taking accountability. Only when we own up to our past, can we let go of it."

*   *   *

Mikey popped out of my mother's belly, a whopping ten pounds, already looking like a five-month-old. His big, blue eyes, round, angelic face and golden hair were reminiscent of a Michelangelo cherub.

"Such a sweet baby. Such a pretty baby," my mother cooed in his ear.

"You weren't a very pretty baby," she told me. "You had jet-black eyes and a furry head."

I was three and a half years old, and all I knew was that blue eyes were better than brown, and mine were brown, and Mikey's were blue, and that was enough reason to hate him.

From the get-go, I was a shitty sister. I didn't play with his chubby fingers or kiss his baby-skin forehead or tell him how happy I was to have such a "pretty" little brother. I spent most of my time thinking about how I could get rid of him.

We were living in a small house that backed up to a canal in Plantation, Florida. I had once seen a manatee in the water and thought it was a monster. I wasn't sure what manatees were, but I was pretty sure they'd like my brother.

When he was six weeks old, my mother left him unattended, strapped tightly in an infant seat in the middle of their king-sized bed, so she could go to the bathroom.

Thump.

Whahhhhhh.

My mother heard him crying and came running out of the bathroom. When she saw me on the bed and my brother on the floor, she screamed, "Kimmi! What did you do?!"

That story was used as proof that I had a mean streak as a child.

For years, I kicked, squeezed and slapped my brother as if he were a doll in a therapist's office, specifically designed to help me get out my anger. "Don't tell Mom," I would say, and he wouldn't. No matter what I did or how mean I was, Mikey would follow me around like a puppy, refusing to tell on me. As a result, this abuse went pretty much unnoticed and unpunished until the summer of '79.

I was seven. Mikey was four. My thirteen-year-old half sister Lisa—from my father's second marriage, the one before the marriage to my mother—had just come to live with us in Tulsa, Oklahoma, jockeying me out of firstborn position and turning me into a middle child overnight. There wasn't less chicken for me to eat. I didn't have to wear hand-me-downs or sleep on a bottom bunk. But the energy in the house shifted.

It was a Sunday afternoon. The house was quiet except for the buzz of summer coming through the open windows. My father was outside trimming the hedges. My mother was reading a book on the kitchen couch. Lisa was upstairs in her bedroom with the door locked. And Mikey and I were playing in the basement.

"Mommy," I cried, running upstairs. "Mikey bit me," I said, extending my arm to show her the bite mark.

"Ohhhh, Kimmi," she said, kissing my arm and hugging me tightly. "Where is your brother?!"

"Downstairs," I whimpered.

My brother was playing with his train set when my mother grabbed his arm and bit it, not hard enough to leave teeth marks, but a good, solid bite. "You are not to bite your sister," she said, waving her finger in his face. "Biting is bad."

"I didn't. I didn't," he screamed and cried, holding his arm to his chest in pain.

"Now go to your room," she commanded.

"Kimmi, are you okay, sweetheart?" she asked, taking my arm into her hand and looking at the bite mark again. "Wait a minute," she said, glaring down at me, noticing the mark was missing two front teeth. "You bit yourself?!"

"I'm sorry, Mommy. I'm sorry."

"I'm getting the wooden spoon," she said, and ran upstairs to the kitchen.

"No, Mommy, no. Please don't," I pleaded. "I'm sorry. I'm sorry."

My mother had threatened us with the wooden spoon before, but had never used it. She threw me over her knee and hit my bottom with the flat end of the spoon three times. "What you did was VERY, VERY, VERY bad." She spent the rest of the day consoling my brother, and I cried myself to sleep that night, hating him even more.

Shortly after the biting incident, my brother started to wheeze. The allergist insisted he carry around an inhaler and get a humidifier for his bedroom. For some reason, his symptoms got worse at night. He would wheeze and cough, clear his throat and cry. My mother would sit on the edge of his bed, rub his tummy with a warm washcloth, and whisper, "Everything's going to be okay, Mikey. Everything's going to be okay." I wished she would say that to me. What had been sibling rivalry turned into war.

I curled my hair with sponge rollers, wore the prettiest, pinkest tutu in the world, danced around and sang, "I'm a curbstone cutie, Mama's pride and beauty, they call me jelly beans!" It didn't make a difference. I couldn't compete with sick. So I peed in Mikey's lemonade. I covered myself in ketchup and pretended to be dead to scare him. I put Cascade in his Coke. I was rotten.

Then the left side of his face puffed out like a blowfish. I thought maybe the Cascade had exploded in his cheek.

When the swelling and pain got worse, Mikey's pediatrician thought it might be cancer. My parents immediately hopped on a plane to New York with my brother to see Dr. Biller at Mount Sinai, leaving Lisa and me with the Gladstones.

The Gladstones weren't bad people. My father worked with Mr. Gladstone, so I knew his face. He was a short, chubby man who was always laughing and slapping my father on the back. His wife was also short and chubby, but she didn't find the world funny. She looked like a mean schoolteacher, the kind who would hit you on the wrist with a ruler for not knowing how to say "strawberry" in French.

I slept on a pullout couch in the basement. I remember it in flashes. *Swiss Family Robinson* playing on the TV in the sunken living room. A dog. A ship. The phone on the wall downstairs. Mrs. Gladstone's hair. The smell of hairspray. And I remember what wasn't there. My mother. My father. I even missed my brother.

Six days felt like a year. For all I knew, they were never coming back and I would have to live the rest of my life in the Gladstones' basement with funny noises and not enough blankets to keep me warm at night.

"Mommy, I'm really sick and Mrs. Gladstone made me go to school," I said, leaning against the wall, pulling on the white phone cord.

"Honey, Mikey needs us," my mother tried to explain.

"*I* need you."

"Honey, Mikey is very sick. He needs us more now. We'll be back soon. I love you, angel baby."

I crawled into bed, sharp springs digging into my back, and I thought maybe if I had been better, this wouldn't be happening. Maybe Mikey wouldn't be in the hospital and my mommy never would have left me.

★   ★   ★

"Justice is about letting go?" I ask Iris for clarification.

"That's part of it. It's also about Karmic debt, which is slightly different. As I said before, it's about righting the wrongs of our past."

"I can't go back and redo my childhood."

"People try to all the time. Most adult relationships involve acting out early childhood drama. We make the same mistakes over and over until we learn forgiveness and compassion. Those are the keys to releasing the past's hold on us."

"I didn't really understand the past's hold on me until a few years ago. I told you about my brother, but I didn't tell you that in April 2003, after we thought his tumors were gone for good, his face started to hurt again. His doctor did a CAT scan, and from everything he saw, he was pretty sure Mikey's tumors had grown back."

★   ★   ★

Noah spent the night at my place the night before the surgery. We weren't in the habit of cuddling like some other couples whose arms and legs intertwine like braided licorice.

228

But on that particular night, he held me close, placing his hand on my head, cradling me like a baby.

Usually, it took two alarms, nine nudges and four are-you-going-to-get-up-nows to wake Noah, but when the alarm clock went off at 6 A.M. with that familiar, chipper rendition of "Here Comes the Sun," he didn't pull his pillow over his head. He rolled over, put his arms around me and said, "I have a good feeling about this. I don't know why, but I know your brother is going to be okay."

We were in a cab by 6:30 A.M. Record time. I threw on jeans and a sweater and was out the door. We were silent, holding hands, as we crossed the park at Ninety-sixth Street on our way to Mount Sinai.

"I can't believe it's been *fifteen* years," I said as we entered the lobby. "The air smells exactly the same." It was a mix of stale bagels, flowers and sick people.

"I hate this smell," Noah said.

I had forgotten he knew it too. He had spent hours, days, weeks in hospitals with *his* brother, who had endured a liver transplant and a kidney transplant due to a rare blood disease. Noah had been through it all with him: good news turned bad news turned good again. His brother had a compromised immune system now and had to be careful, but was living a pretty normal life with a beautiful wife and a baby on the way. I wanted the same for my brother. I wanted to see him grow old with kids.

"Thank you for being here," I said, burying my face in Noah's neck.

"Of course. Just don't hot-breath me," he said, pushing

me away, laughing. He hated when I breathed on his neck or in his ear. It tickled him.

We joined the rest of my family in the waiting area. My mother was talking to the nurse. Her best friend, Susan, was standing at her side. My father was with his wife, also named Susan. Everyone had someone, except Miki, my brother's girlfriend, a dark-haired beauty from Israel, who, yes, had almost the same name as my brother.

Noah handed Miki the green healing stone someone had given him during his brother's kidney transplant. "This might help," he said. "It helped me."

"Thank you," she said, holding the stone close to her chest, her forehead crinkled. She looked delicate despite the buckles and straps on her black top, and the safety pin "laces" on her sneakers.

My brother was in pre-op. We had a long day ahead of us.

"I'm going on a coffee run," my father said. "Want some?"

"A latte, please," I said.

"Nothing, thanks," Noah said.

An hour later . . .

"I'm going on a coffee run," my father said. "Want some?"

"A latte, please," I said.

"Nothing, thanks," Noah said, and looked at me. "I think you should stop drinking coffee."

"You're right," I said, and took a deep breath, realizing my leg hadn't stopped shaking for the last thirty minutes.

"Let's go for a walk. Get some fresh air," Noah said, grabbing my hand. A walk was just what I needed.

Noah and I entered Central Park and headed down a paved pathway until we reached a bench and sat down. The budding tree branches swaying in the spring air made me happy, hopeful even. Noah opened his notebook and started to draw the tree standing in front of us.

"How do you do that?" I asked, so he gave me a mini-lesson in shading.

"You can't just go from dark to light," he said, coloring in the trunk with his pen. "In order for it to look round, you actually have to make the very edge of the dark side a little lighter and the very edge of the light side a little darker," he instructed, going back and adding a few extra lines to the light side.

"I love you," I said.

"I love you too," he said.

I didn't care that I said it first. It felt right.

When we got back to the waiting area, everyone was gone. I called my mother's cell phone—even though you're not supposed to use them in hospitals—and found out that they had moved upstairs to Michael's private room to wait for him there.

My father was pacing. His wife, Susan, was knitting. The other Susan was sitting next to my mother, who was sitting by the phone, talking to Miki, who was curled up on the bed, still holding the healing stone.

I wanted Doritos. Oreos would have been okay too.

"This is a disaster," my father blurted out, his face

231

turning red, his fists shaking, as if he were a cartoon pot of boiling water. "It's been three hours. Why haven't we heard anything?!"

"I'll find out what's going on," Noah said, and left the room.

"He's a good one, Kimmi," my mother said, and then looked at my father. "He's the kind of man you want around."

I got up and ran after him. Together we went down to the second floor to find out what was going on.

"They finished twenty minutes ago. You just missed the doctor," the nurse said, closing her eyes in disapproval. "He was here. Now he's not."

Noah and I raced back upstairs to tell everyone that Michael was out of surgery, but that we didn't know anything more. My mother jumped up. Miki rolled off the bed. They went to find Michael in post-op. The rest of us paced up and down the hallway.

What if he was paralyzed? What if his tumors were no longer benign? What if he had cancer? *Please God, make him be okay.*

Fifteen minutes later, a nurse carted my brother toward us, my mother, Miki and Dr. Urken trailing behind. I hated the creaking sound of the gurney, and the gauze they used to wrap my brother's face. When I was a girl, I thought he looked like a blood-soaked mummy and didn't want to go near him. Now, I wanted to go back in time to kiss his sweet, little face and tell him how happy I am to have him as my baby brother.

"What happened?!" my father demanded, wanting answers NOW.

The nurse ignored my father and continued to wheel my brother into his room. As she made the sharp left, my brother's right arm fell out from underneath the sheet, exposing the huge tattoo he had managed to keep from my father for a good five years.

"What the hell is that?" my father asked.

"Don't worry about it. Just get the door," I said.

Dr. Urken—Dr. Biller's protégé—asked us to follow him inside. His light brown mustache surprised me—total Tom Selleck throwback—but his face was serious and smart and his eyes were kind. He spoke softly and calmly, the way I imagined a monk would speak—also surprising. "Scar tissue," he said.

"Scar tissue," my father repeated.

"I removed fifteen years of built-up scar tissue. He's going to be fine."

We all exhaled at the same time. I looked around the room. Each of us had scar tissue of some sort, years of built up pain and fear that still lingered in our hearts. As the doctor turned to go, I wanted to stop him and ask him if he could remove mine too.

*   *   *

"My brother ended up being fine, but I wasn't fine," I say to Iris. "Being back in the hospital brought up a lot of stuff for me. My brother and I actually got into a really big fight afterward. Something to do with his dogs. He wanted me to take care of them and I didn't want to. It obviously had nothing to do with the dogs. I think I was still holding on to all my jealousy and guilt, and he was upset because he felt like I was never there for him, and I wasn't. We didn't talk for a couple of months. We're slowly making our way back now."

Iris gets out of her chair and heads over to the bookshelf. "Where are you?" she says to the book she's looking for. "Oh, yes! There you are!" She takes it off the shelf and flips to the exact page she's looking for. "Here we go," Iris says, clearing her throat. "'I wondered if that was how forgiveness budded, not with the fanfare of epiphany, but with pain gathering its things, packing up and slipping away unannounced in the middle of the night.'" Iris looks up from the book and raises her eyebrows, as if to say, *Isn't that fucking amazing?* "If you haven't already, you must read *The Kite Runner.* Khaled Hosseini is a phenomenal writer."

Pain slipping away unannounced.

"Can I go back to the Devil for a second?" I ask Iris.

"Of course," she says, and sits back down, resuming her favorite position: right foot tucked under left calf.

"I kept thinking the 'darkness' I had to integrate was shame about sex, that my good-girl stuff was wrapped up in that. I think it might have more to do with love. Like, somehow, after pushing my guilt down for so many years, it took on a life of its own, and as you were saying, acted out in my adult relationships with men, making me feel undeserving of love."

I'm so proud of this insight; I want a gold star.

"We see things in layers. I'm sure you'll see this reading

very differently when you leave. The cards will take on new meaning the more you live. That's how it goes. Have you ever seen a movie as a kid and then seen it later as an adult and said to yourself, 'Oh, *that's* what that was about?' We can only see what we're ready to see at the time. That's what I love about the cards. You could come back in ten years, get the same cards and have a completely different reading."

"But in *this* reading, you said Justice is what I want but fear most?"

"Yes. You want resolution. You want to move on, let go of old feelings that hold you back, but you're scared. You're afraid you won't be forgiven, that you don't deserve to be forgiven."

La Templanza / La Tempérance
Arcana: XIIII
Path on Kabbalah Tree of Life: 25
Color: Blue
Astrological sign: Sagittarius
Constellation: Aquarius
Musical note: G Sharp

chapter eleven
temperance

"The task we must set for ourselves is not to feel secure, but
to be able to tolerate insecurity."
—ERICH FROMM

"Temperance, your final outcome card—"

"Wait," I interrupt, "but I feel like I'm just beginning
to understand."

"It's not over just yet," she says. "Temperance represents healing at the deepest level. With *time*, we are able to
find compassion for ourselves and others. We can see past
pain and injustice with a kinder, wiser heart. This is the
last card in your spread. It means all roads lead here. This,
Kimberlee, is what you've been working toward."

I feel chills run up my spine and the hairs on my arms stand on end. Something about Iris's voice in this moment makes me feel as if she's handing me the Holy Grail. I look at the card. An angel with glorious red wings stands at the edge of crystal-clear water, radiating the light of the sun behind her. She holds a gold goblet in each hand, passing water back and forth between the two, forming a steady stream. "There's something incredibly peaceful about this card," I say.

"Water can be very healing. It cleanses us. Soothes us. And symbolically, when water is exchanged in equal proportions, moderation and balance can be achieved, extremes eradicated, and harmony found."

"Irises," I say, pointing to the flowers in the picture.

"Indeed," Iris says, and smiles with pride.

"Don't you think it means—Ah, right. We see what we want to see."

★ ★ ★

The first time I sat down on Noah's toilet to pee, I couldn't take my eyes off of a framed picture hanging on the wall across from me. It wasn't a 5 × 7 class photo like the one Zach displayed on his desk. It wasn't the size of a Farrah Fawcett poster, like the one hanging above Daniel's bed. It was small and looked like a tic-tac-toe game. In each box, instead of an X or O, a straw wreath framed another face. I flushed the toilet, got up and squinted to get a better look. I was drawn to a woman in one of the boxes. I couldn't tell whether she was a blonde or a redhead. It didn't matter. She had light skin, big blue eyes and a wide smile. I knew where she fell on the pretty scale.

"Hey, who's this?" I asked, dragging Noah into the bathroom.

"Silke."

"The girl you visited in Germany before we met?"

"Yeah, that one."

"The one you were on and off with for three years?"

"Yeah."

"You're still friends?"

"Yes, Kimberlee, we're still friends," he said, leaving the bathroom. "I'm not in love with her anymore, if that's what you're worried about, but I'll always love her."

Not what I wanted to hear.

Every time I spent the night at his place, I would stare at her picture and try to imagine what she looked like without that damn wreath. I wanted to see other pictures of her, but there was never a good opportunity.

"Are you sure you don't want to go with me to the video store?" Noah asked me one night.

"No, I'll stay here," I said. "Whatever looks good to you."

"Chicken Milanese fine?" he asked.

"Yeah, chicken is great."

Noah shut the door behind him, locked it, checked it twice and then jogged downstairs and out the door. I peeped through the peephole to make sure he was gone, ran over to his bookcase, took his photo albums off the shelf and carried them to the bed. Then, like a dog that has gotten into a bag of kibbles, I dove in headfirst, scrutinizing each picture.

The albums were chronological, starting with child-hood. I breezed through those shots. I wanted to see what his first love, Jenny, looked like. All I knew about her was that she had long blond hair down to her butt. And there she was. I found her. She and Noah were sit-ting next to each other at a Passover seder. Noah was pointing at the Haggadah. She was looking at him, smil-ing. She was much prettier than Zach's ex-girlfriend Maggie, the one I had obsessed over for years, and defi-nitely prettier than Daniel's ex-girlfriend Juliette, which wasn't that hard to be. I thought I'd be more upset at the sight of her, but she didn't threaten me. Maybe because I knew she and Noah were no longer in touch and that she had gotten married.

Silke, on the other hand, bothered the shit out of me. Turned out she was a blonde, not a redhead, and much pret-tier than the picture in the bathroom had led me to believe. In one shot, she was standing next to the rocky edge of a mountain wearing a tank top and shorts, a sweatshirt wrapped around her waist. Her nipples were standing at at-tention and I couldn't stop staring at them. I thought back to something Noah had said: "Silke was really comfortable in her skin." I wasn't comfortable in my skin. I picked my skin. *Fucking bitch.*

There were all kinds of pictures—pictures from par-ties, pictures of family events, weddings, trips abroad—but I only lingered on the ex-girlfriends, flipping through the rest quickly. As I stared at another picture of Silke with a tiny flower tucked behind her ear, wishing I had a magnifying glass, I wondered if I'd be pasted on a page in one of these albums one day, if his next girlfriend, or wife, would look at *me* with envy.

Sitting on his bed, albums scattered, pictures out of plastic sleeves, imagining life without him before we even had a chance to have a life together, I noticed the clock.

7:30 P.M.

Shit. Shit. Shit.

He would be back any minute.

Just as I placed the last album back on the shelf, I heard the downstairs door slam. The way sound traveled in his building was insane—cardboard would provide better insulation. Footsteps. I sat on the edge on the bed, crossed my legs and acted as if I had been twiddling my thumbs.

"Hey, babe," he said, opening the door.

"Hey," I said, wondering if he'd be able to see in my face what I had just done.

"I couldn't find *Wings of Desire*, so I got *The Harder They Come*."

I would have watched *The Terminator*. I didn't care. I wanted to erase the movies playing in my head.

"Thanks for getting dinner," I said, grabbing the takeout bag so I could set up plates for us.

We sat on Noah's bed, eating breaded chicken cutlets and crispy potatoes, and watched Jimmy Cliff bounce around Jamaica trying to become a Reggae superstar. Afterward, Noah poured himself a Bushmills whiskey neat and I pretended I wasn't still thinking about Silke's nipples.

★   ★   ★

"We see what we want to see and what we're ready to see," Iris says. "One way we can start seeing through a new lens is by putting ourselves in situations that remind us of the past or who we used to be. If we never give ourselves the chance to prove we've changed, how will we ever know we have?"

"I put myself in the most uncomfortable situation imaginable, scarier than jumping out of a plane, scarier than being left alone in the jungle for a month. . . . I met Noah's ex-girlfriend."

"You're going to have to explain why meeting Noah's ex-girlfriend was scarier than jumping out of a plane, because frankly, that seems pretty terrifying to me," Iris says.

"Are you afraid of heights?" I ask.

"Not necessarily, but plummeting to earth with a parachute that may or may not open—"

"Do I detect a little *fear*?" I ask, and flash an impish smile.

"I *am* human," she says, and crosses her arms over her chest.

"You just seem so strong to me, like you've conquered fear."

"I prefer adventures of the heart. You won't find me climbing Mount Everest."

"Yeah, I couldn't really imagine that. But if you told me you swam with sharks, it wouldn't surprise me."

"You're the one who swims with sharks." Iris says, a smile creeping back onto her face.

"I shouldn't have told you that," I say, and laugh.

Sage, her black cat, saunters back into the room and jumps onto my lap.

"Hello," I say, and scratch the backs of his ears.

"So tell me. Why was meeting Silke scarier than jumping out of a plane?"

★   ★   ★

I grabbed Noah's arm for warmth. It was our second winter together, and we were walking back to his apartment from brunch.

"Silke's coming to town," he said, looking straight ahead.

"I'm invited, right?" It was more a statement than a question.

"Yeah, sure. Do you really want to come, though?"

No, I don't really want to come. I just don't want you to go without me.

"When is she coming?" I asked.

"In a couple weeks," he said, opening the door.

"How long have you known?" I asked.

"For a while," he said. "I thought you'd be upset."

When we got back to his apartment, I threw my coat onto his bed in a huff.

"Kimberlee, she's my friend."

A friend you used to fuck.

The morning we were supposed to meet Silke for brunch, Noah reached over and started caressing my breasts.

I had gotten zero sleep. The last thing I wanted to do was get busy. His hand moved down. We had sex. It was different somehow. Quiet, tender, reassuring.

"You don't have to go," he said one more time before we left.

"I'm okay," I said, feeling better having his scent on me.

I wore a gray and black pinstriped wool miniskirt along with a gray turtleneck sweater, black opaque tights, and boots. My hair was shorter than I liked it to be, but I managed to fluff it up. I liked that Noah didn't make a fuss about what he looked like. It seemed like a good sign.

We got into a cab and headed over to Friend of a Farmer, a cute little restaurant on Irving Place with homemade honey wheat bread and jams.

The hostess escorted us upstairs and motioned to a corner table against the back wall.

"That's perfect," I said, and scooted all the way in. A wall behind me. A wall to my left. Noah to my right.

"You okay?" Noah asked, taking my hand under the table and squeezing it.

"Yeah," I said.

I was far from okay. My teeth were tingling. My hands were sweating. My knees were knocking together.

Noah's eyes widened.

A woman with blond hair was ascending the stairs. At first, only the golden white crown of her head was visible, then her profile, then she turned. She was in full view now. Noah stood up and smiled. I stood up, my face fake and stiff.

"Hi," Noah called out.

The woman looked at us blankly. "I'm sorry. I don't know you," she said, and turned to find her friends.

How do you mistake a woman you dated for three years with someone else?

"That was weird," Noah said, his upper lip curled.

"I'll say," I said, and exhaled, happy to have survived the initial adrenaline rush.

We sat back down, looking like Gogo and Didi in *Waiting for Godot,* sitting stiffly in our chairs, facing out, side by side, scratching our heads, biting our nails.

Then we saw it. Another white crown. A profile. Silke. She got to the top of the stairs and turned toward us. Her hair was long and straight, different from the pictures I had seen of her. It was still shiny, and her face was still angelic.

We stood up again, laughing nervously. "You'll never believe it," Noah started to say, and pointed to the woman he had mistaken her for. "We thought that was you." Silke giggled. I was pretty sure she didn't find it funny.

I shook her hand. *My* skin against *her* skin.

She was no longer a girl in a picture hanging on Noah's bathroom wall. She was in front of me—alive and breathing—a real human being in jeans and a long-sleeved blue sweater.

Noah and I sat back down. Again. Silke paused. The open place setting was in front of Noah, but she moved it over and sat across from me. She was right in front of me. I could play footsie with her, if I wanted to. Her sweater was bulky, so I couldn't see her nipples, but I stared at her mouth and imagined Noah kissing her. Her lips were soft and supple. Mine were chapped.

At first, the conversation was formal.

"How long are you in town?"

"Why are you here?"

"The granola is very good."

Then it got personal, as it does with me. I wasn't sure if it was her trembling hands, or the way her gentle voice cracked when she spoke, but I found myself telling her about my mother's sexual abuse and my brother's surgery and my father's new life in philadelphia.

Her eyes were open and listening. I knew you could tell a lot about a person by looking into their eyes—the windows to the soul and all—but I didn't know eyes could hear. Hers could, and I understood why Noah had loved her, why he still loved her.

The waitress came over and asked if we wanted coffee refills.

"Hey, isn't this . . . ," Silke started to say, and stopped herself.

I knew what she was going to say: "Isn't this like the mug you have at home?"

Noah had the same exact coffee cup, except his was white with one blue stripe instead of two. I wanted to touch her hand to let her know I knew she was being considerate, I knew she was trying not to bring up the past or hurt me with her intimate knowledge of him.

In that moment, I felt connected to her. I liked that we

both knew what his dishes looked like and how much he loved coffee and how he got grumpy on an empty stomach, and how sometimes he could be stubborn and arrogant, but when he was open, there wasn't a purer heart in the world.

I smiled.

She smiled back.

I couldn't believe it. I liked her. I liked her a lot.

Noah asked about her family and work and then told her about his family and work. I was happy they had stuff to catch up on, which meant he hadn't been sneaking into the other room at night to call her; they hadn't been trading weekly emails with emotional updates and sexual innuendoes. It was clear they still cared for each other and wanted to know the other was all right in the world, and I loved them both for that.

The brunch crowd, including Silke's doppelganger, slowly filtered out. It was getting late, so Noah paid the check.

When we got outside, I reached over to give Silke a hug good-bye. As I leaned in, the sunlight exposed the fragility and transparency of her skin.

When I was a little girl, my favorite book was *The Monster at the End of the Book,* in which Grover from *Sesame Street* is told there's a monster at the end of the book. He is absolutely terrified and BEGS you not to turn the page. He nails boards together, he builds brick walls, he ties down pages with rope, but nothing works. You keep turning the pages and he must face the inevitable . . . that *he* is the monster at the end of the book.

I hugged Silke and realized I was Grover.

★　★　★

"At first, I wasn't sure why I was so scared to meet Silke," I say to Iris. "I thought maybe I wouldn't be able to handle how pretty she was. What would I do if she and Noah were still in love? But you're right, meeting her showed me how much I had changed. I'm no longer the little girl who can't compete with her sick brother. I don't have to compete for love. There's enough to go around."

"Hallelujah," Iris says. "People often avoid situations they think will make them feel bad, but taking responsibility for one's feelings means responding honestly in the moment, which sounds like what you did. You surprised yourself and proved to yourself that you were stronger than you knew. Usually, I don't do this . . ." Iris picks up the deck and flips through it, pulling out a card and handing it to me.

The woman in the card is naked and alone, free-floating in space, with a wide purple ribbon wrapped strategically around her. Earlier in the night, I would have been convinced that because *she* was alone, it meant I was going to be alone too, and that Noah would ultimately say "no" to me.

"I don't know why," I say, "but this card reminds me of something Rilke said about marriage," I say, and hold up the card. "I'm going to totally butcher it, something like, 'Marriage is not a hemming in or a tearing down of all boundaries.'" I look up to the ceiling to remember what goes next. " 'That the merging of two people is an impossibility, so if we learn how to accept the distance between even the closest people, then we can see each other as whole against an immense sky.' "

"That's one of my favorite quotes on marriage," Iris says, clasping her hands together. "Well, that and what Martin Buber said about the pitfalls of romantic love."

"Why do you want me to look at this?" I ask.

"That is for you to discover on your own. The World represents the end of a cycle. A lesson learned."

"What if I don't figure it out?" I ask.

"You've done such good work up until this point. I know you will." Iris gets up from her chair and comes to sit on the edge of mine. Sage jumps off my lap and flies out of the room. Iris puts her hand on my shoulder. The heat from her skin sends waves of warm fuzzies throughout my body. "Everything's going to be okay," she says.

"Thank you," I say, tearing up. "I needed that."

"Do you want me to get you a car service?" she asks.

"Actually, I'd really love to use your bathroom. All that iced tea," I say, and put my hand on my bladder. I stand up and feel stiff. I look at the clock. It's midnight. "Wow. It's only been two hours. I feel like we've been together for a week," I say.

"Maybe we have," she says, lifting the tray with our empty iced tea glasses and lemon-snap cookie crumbs on it. "This way," she says, walking toward the kitchen.

I follow her down the dark hallway and notice a painting of her as a younger woman on the wall, lounging naked on a couch, kind of like *The Grand Odalisque* woman with an elongated back, looking over her shoulder.

"That's you?" I ask in amazement.

"My husband was good with his hands."

Your husband couldn't have been Ingres. You're not that old.

Iris inclines her head to the right. "The bathroom is that way. Make sure to put the cover down when you finish. Sage loves to get wet."

I open the door and feel around for the light. It's a dimmer. I slide it up. It's a small bathroom, more of a powder room, really. The walls are the color of my favorite Crayola crayon: pacific blue. The sink is set into a beautifully ornate dresser with brass handles and wood inlay. There is a mirror framed with gold leaf garlands. On each side, there are sconces that look ancient, as if they should hold candles, not lightbulbs. I notice the hand towels are crisp and pristine.

I was right. She irons her linens.

I sit on the toilet and stare at the blue walls, still thinking about the World card.

Soaping up my hands, letting the cool water slip through my fingers, I smile at my face in the mirror—so different from a couple of weeks ago at Morton's Steakhouse, holding my breath, wiping mascara from my face, not sure what to say to my father.

As I head back to the living room, Iris taps me on the shoulder. I jump.

"You scared me," I say, and laugh.

"Spooooky," Iris sings.

"And you sure like to sing," I say.

"I'm a singer," Iris says, and walks ahead of me, continuing to sing, "with a Spooooky little girl like you."

"Professionally?" I ask.

"I believe we are what we do . . . I happen to sing," she says and does a little twirl.

"And dance?"

"No, not really. Although I was thinking about signing up for a dance class at Steps. What do you think?"

Whoa. Are you asking me *a question?*

"I think that sounds like a good idea."

"Well," Iris says. "It's been an honor, Kimberlee."

"Thank you," I say, and reach for my bag. I open my wallet, take out $75 and hand it to her. "Exact change, how do you like that? So, when should I come back?"

"I hope you don't," Iris says with a chuckle.

"Don't you see people on a regular basis? I know my friend Karen has been here several times."

"Each person is different. I think you need to stop going to other people for the answers."

"Well, then. I guess I won't be seeing you again."

"Maybe just not in the way you think," she says, and walks me to the door. We're halfway down the hallway when Iris says, "Oh, wait." She rushes back into the living room. "I meant for you to have this, not simply to look at it," she says, coming back and handing me the World card.

"But doesn't that mess up your deck?"

"I have hundreds of decks," she says. "I want you to have it. I want you to hold on to it. Meditate on it. It's the last of the twenty-two Major Arcana. You're close, Kimberlee. You're very close."

Iris opens the door.

"Would you mind if I gave you a hug?" I ask.

"I'd love a hug," Iris says, and gets up on her tiptoes.

I bend down to meet her and hug her tight. I count in my head to see who lets go first. *One. Two. Three. Four.* She's not going to let go. *Five. Six.* I release my hands from her back and smile. "Thank you for that," I say, and kiss her on the cheek.

"You are more than welcome. Now remember . . ."

"What?" I ask, as if I've forgotten a homework assignment I didn't know I had in the first place.

"Breathe," she says, and inhales deeply, opening her arms to let in the air.

"You got it," I say, smile and take a deep breath.

She waves me off and shuts the door.

Poof. She's gone.

As I walk back down the stairs, I wonder about her daughter and her late husband and her singing and how she can afford such a nice apartment and then I laugh at myself. *Why can't I be fine with not knowing? What's wrong with a little mystery?*

I reach the front door and peer out the window before opening it. The street looks as empty as it did before. I figure

I'll have to walk to Broadway to get a cab. I step outside and I'm enveloped by the sweet, late summer air.

I skip down the steps and blow a kiss good-bye to the lions.

Just then, a cab rounds the corner. The light on its roof is on.

Score.

THE WORLD.

El Mundo / Le Monde
Arcana: XXI
Path on Kabbalah Tree of Life: 32
Color: Blue-Violet or Indigo
Astrological sign: Saturn
Constellation: Lesser Bear and Pole Star
Musical note: A

epilogue
the world

"Round and round and round in the circle game."
—JONI MITCHELL

It's too late to call Noah when I get home from Iris's. What would I tell him anyway? A tarot reader gave me the World. Who needs marriage now? That wouldn't be the truth. I still want to get married, but something inside me feels different.

I crawl into bed and roll over onto my side. When I close my eyes, I see flashes of Iris's face. Her nose. Her lips. Her eyes. Images from the cards pop into my head. The crescent moon. The Grim Reaper's smile. A sword. The balance scale. Sage, Iris's cat, jumps onto the High Priestess's lap and startles me. I flip onto my back, take a few deep breaths and feel Iris slowly slip away.

The next morning, I wake up to "Here Comes the Sun," as usual, and know what I have to do. I have to call my father. First I have to take a shower and go to work, but then I have to ask my dad for a "sit-down."

"I really want to see you," I say.

"I'm very busy," he says. Busy means business. Busy means golf. Busy means dinner with friends, travel with his wife, the TV show *24*. "Let me figure something out and I'll let you know."

A couple of weeks later my father calls and says, "Okay. New Jersey. I know a great Italian place. Best Veal Parmesan around. You like veal, don't you?"

Who admits to liking baby cow? But sure, I won't deny it, I like a good Veal Parm.

"Yeah, Dad. Veal sounds good."

"Wednesday at seven it is, then!"

"What if I had other plans?" I ask.

"Do you?"

"No," I say.

"Then fine. I'll email you the address when I get to the office. It's in a strip mall. Should be pretty easy to find."

"A strip mall in New Jersey, how fancy."

"It is one of the best restaurants around," he says, as if I've just insulted his dog.

"I'm sure I'll love it. I would eat at McDonald's if it meant getting to see you."

"Awww," he says, and gets off the phone.

Wednesday at 6:30 P.M., I cross the George Washington Bridge and call my mother from the car my father gave me after September 11. "Hey, Mom. I'm on my way to meet Dad for dinner and think I might be on the wrong road. Can you Google-Map for me? It's 108 Chestnut Hill Road, in Montvale and I just turned onto Route 17."

"You're about fifteen minutes away," my mother says in her comforting voice, a voice that beats the hell out of the GPS turn-left-at-the-light electronic voice.

"I'm so nervous."

"It's not hard. There are only a few more turns."

"No, I'm nervous to talk to Dad."

"He just wants you to be happy," my mother says. "We all want you to be happy. You're our baby girl." I don't feel like such a baby at thirty-three. But then again, I'm on the phone with my mother, still wanting her to help me get from here to there.

She stays on the phone with me and talks me through the rest of the trip until I see the restaurant. "Okay, honey bunny, good luck. Your father loves you."

I pull into the lot and park. It looks like average suburbia. Cars. Cement. More cars. I could be anywhere in America. But when I walk inside the restaurant, it's a scene straight out of *The Sopranos*. Round men stuffing their faces. Women with big hair, big tits and too much makeup. And my father, who has already ordered wine, sitting with his back to the wall, facing out, wearing yet another monogrammed shirt.

"Kimma," he says, and smiles wide, his eyes sparkling.

In person, there's an aliveness in my father I don't get over the phone. I always forget how much I like him.

I kiss him on the cheek and get the one-handed pat he's famous for in my family.

"You look good," he says, more chipper than usual.

Something's up.

"You do too," I say.

"I got a pinkie ring," he says, and holds up his hand to show me.

I burst into laughter and then whisper, "You are so Mafioso. Are you going to have people kiss it?"

"I love jewelry," he says, and admires it.

My father, the Metrosexual.

He slips it off and hands it to me to try on. It fits my ring finger. I immediately move it to my middle finger.

"It's beautiful. And heavy," I say, handing it back to him.

"A lot of men from my generation wear pinkie rings."

"Well, it looks nice on you," I say, noticing its roundness, its thickness, how the Ceylon sapphire is set deeply into the gold and how the diamonds on each side make it look like one big eye staring up at him. I twist the ring Noah gave me and take a breath. I want to tell my father the story, but I know he won't get it.

On my first anniversary with Noah, we stayed at the Hudson Hotel, where we had met for our first date. We flopped onto the crisp white sheets and exchanged presents. I went first. I handed him a memory book. I had pasted our JDate profiles and pictures, email exchanges, and photocopies of sexy paintings I had taken from an art book called *Erotic Art*. He flipped through the pages with tears in his eyes. Then it was his turn. He handed me a little black box. I knew he wasn't proposing. He had been telling me about the ring for a while. I opened the box slowly. "Oh, Noah, I love it!" "Infinite Breath," he called it. "A ring to remind you to breathe." Two strands of white gold wrapping around each other, never broken, but opening twice to form the sign of infinity, with a Burmese ruby in each of the infinity sign's holes. It looked like the eyes of the Buddha. I loved it, and I loved that I had found a man who wanted me to breathe and relax and be myself.

The waiter shuffles over to our table and asks us if we're ready to order.

"So whatcha gonna have?" my father asks me.

"You said the Veal Parm is good. I think I'll have that."

"Me too," he says.

We sip wine as he tells me about my half sister Lisa's kids, my half brother David's kids, my stepbrother Ace's kids. The way he talks about his grandchildren makes me sad. I'm sad that he didn't spend that kind of time with us as kids, and I'm sad I haven't given him grandchildren yet. Even though I'm still on the fence about kids, leaning more toward wanting them than not, in this moment, I want them for sure. I want to see his face glow when he talks about my children too.

"So," I say.

"So?" he asks, and grins.

"About Noah."

"I said my peace," he says, and pats his palms on the table. "I wasn't going to say anything tonight. Not one word. I was going to be a good boy."

"Dad, we really need to talk." My father's face is open, more so than usual. His eyes widen, waiting for me to speak. "Are you ashamed of me?" I ask. "Is it embarrassing when your friends ask you how I'm doing and you have to say that I'm not married, I don't have kids, I don't own property? Does that embarrass you?"

"No!" he says, thrusting his head back, making his double chin more pronounced. "I don't want you to get married for the sake of being married. I want you to be happy."

"Okay," I say, believing him. "You say you're mad at Noah, but do you think you're really mad at me? For screwing up my life and not making the right choices?"

"I thought about that. I thought maybe I was mad at you. But, no. I'm mad at Noah. I don't understand what he's waiting for."

"Dad, I keep telling you, Noah is good to me. I love him more than anyone on this planet. He's helped me like myself more. I've really grown and learned to trust because of him."

"Character is based on how we make decisions. If Noah is able to make this commitment, he'll be a good partner for you. If he can't, then I worry for my daughter."

"I know, Dad. But your time frame is different from mine, and I can't break up with Noah just because *you* think I should, or because you think he'll come back to me if I do. This is my life and I have to live it. I'm the one who has to wake up in the morning and be okay with—"

"I know you do. But I'm afraid you're going to pretend you don't want the things you want in life. If I believed in my heart you would be happy without marriage and kids, that would be one thing, but I don't buy it."

The waiter interrupts us. "Watch out, this plate is very, very hot."

The mammoth piece of veal in front of me takes up the entire plate. I can barely see the spaghetti underneath.

"Bon appetit," my father says.

I cut a piece and scoop up the cheese with my knife, piling it onto the fork. I take a bite. It's delicious. I feel guilty, not only because I'm eating a baby cow, but also because there must be five hundred calories in this one bite alone.

"Do you think you can protect me from hurt?" I ask, lifting up my glass of water to wash down the cheese.

"I'd like to be able to," he says with an unfamiliar softness in his voice.

"Dad, you can't protect me. I could get married and divorced. I could have a sick kid, God forbid. Anything can happen. What you need to trust is that I can deal with my pain. I'm strong. I will make bad choices and good choices, and things will happen to me, and I will happen to things." As he's looking at me, kind of in shock, I realize I've never spoken this way to him before. I may never have spoken this way to anyone before.

"I understand," he says.

My father and I spend the next several minutes chowing down on cheese and meat and perfectly cooked spaghetti.

The waiter tries to pour us more wine, but my father sticks his hand over the mouth of the bottle and says, "No, I want my daughter to take this home with her. But I would like a cappuccino and some biscotti," my father says.

I swear, if I didn't know my father was Jewish, I'd think he was Italian. His silver, pouffy hair. His dark brown eyes. The way he dresses. How much he loves biscotti.

"Chamomile tea," I say, and smile at the waiter.

My father's BlackBerry buzzes. He checks to see who's calling.

"There's something I need from you, Dad."

"Anything," he says, placing his phone down.

"I need you to bless us," I say. "I believe in negative and positive energy, and I can't stand the idea of you sending hateful thoughts into the Universe about someone I love. I need you to want us to work out. Whether or not we end up walking down the aisle, I need your support."

"I can do that," he says, his eyes glassy.

When I get back to the city, I call Noah.

Noah has been a good sport. He likes my father. He thought it was inappropriate for him to get me an engagement ring, but other than that, he thinks my father is a "marshmallow." What exactly that means, I don't know. I think it has something to do with the fact that underneath it all, my father has a kind heart and wants to do good.

"How did it go?" Noah asks.

"It went well," I say. "I got him to bless us."

Silence.

"Isn't that good?" I ask.

"You're an emotional superhero," he says.

Noah and I say good night and hang up the phone.

As I lie underneath the covers, I can feel my body buzz. There's a power in me. It's as if Malvina has become me or I have become her. I have taken the reins. I have stopped playing the victim. Noah, this life, it's all my choice and I can choose differently as time goes by.

I walk into work the next day as if it's any other day, but it's not. Somehow even my job isn't so bad anymore. Sure, it's not what I want to be doing, but the basement walls no longer feel like a prison once I see that I'm there of my own volition. No one is holding me down. I even kind of understand why I've stayed all this time. It's the panic. The threat of breaking news. I picked a place to work that echoed my childhood. I grew up afraid. It's what I'm used to.

I smile at my boss. I smile at the guards in the lobby on my way to lunch. I smile at the guy from Pod B who always asks stupid questions. My smile is my freedom, and seeing it this way makes me smile more.

It's Thursday afternoon and I have to get a flu shot. We're going to Noah's family's house for Rosh Hashanah in a few weeks and we can't be around Noah's brother if we haven't been vaccinated. I go upstairs and stand in line with twenty other people.

"You sure seem happy," a guy from the radio department says.

"Yeah, I am," I say.

"It's nice to see."

"It's nice to feel."

It's my turn. I sit down across from the doctor and explain Noah's brother's situation, the organ transplants, his compromised immune system. She asks me if I'm allergic to eggs. I say no. She gives me a shot and I head back downstairs to the newsroom.

After work I go home, jump in the shower, put on makeup, get dressed and wait for Noah downstairs. We're heading to Brooklyn for a friend's dinner party. He pulls up in the car. We smile at each other the same way we did when we first met. It's instantaneous.

"Ready to eat some delicious chicken with nutmeg?" Noah says, shifting into drive.

"You betcha," I say.

We cross the park at Sixty-sixth Street and head down Second Avenue. Noah suddenly pulls over to the right-hand side of the road in front of a liquor shop and puts on the hazards. "I forgot the wine. Be right back," he says, and hops out.

I flip through the radio and land on Bobby McFerrin's song "Don't Worry, Be Happy." I think back to the 80s and my big hair and all the traveling, and suddenly feel the right side of my head fall asleep. I've had my foot turn to pins and needles before, but never my head. I slap my face a few times, trying to make it stop, to get the blood circulating, but the tingling only gets worse.

Noah comes out of the store and sees me slapping my face through the window.

"Uh, what's going on?" he asks as he fastens his seat belt.

"My face feels weird and tingly."

"Really? Do you feel the tingling in your extremities?"

"Is my head an extremity?"

"Not exactly. Do you feel it in your arms and legs?" he asks.

"Well, kind of. Maybe. I don't know. Why?!"

"When I got my flu shot, the nurse told me if you feel numbness in your extremities, you should go to the emergency room immediately. There's some rare virus you can get from the flu shot. Something-Barr syndrome."

"I already have Epstein-Barr."

"It's something else. G-something syndrome. Call your mom and have her Google it," Noah says, and heads back down Second Avenue.

"Mom, hi. My head feels numb. I got a flu shot today and Noah thinks I may have some weird virus. Can you Google it?"

"Jesus, Kimmi. Let me get to my computer."

I feel the sensation making its way up my legs. Then my arms start to go numb.

"Noah, it's in my extremities! It's making its way up my extremities!"

"Guillain-Barré syndrome," my mother says and gasps. "Respirator. Paralysis. Omigod. Kimmi!"

Completely unable to deal, I hand the phone to Noah.

"Yes, Loryn. I understand, Loryn. We're on our way."

Noah hangs up the phone and turns to me, while still managing to keep an eye on the road and the cabs driving around like bumper cars. In a soft, reassuring voice he says, "I'm taking you to the emergency room. I'm sure there's nothing to worry about. You know, anxiety can make these things worse, so breathe. Keep breathing," he says, and steps on the gas.

"Paralysis?" I say, slapping the back of my head.

"Don't even think about it," he says.

He drops me off at Beth Israel Medical Center and goes to park the car.

I run in.

Thank God my legs still work.

"Emergency room?" I ask the security guard.

"Follow the yellow line," he says, and points.

Behind the glass partition, two women sit at desks. One is thumbing through files. The other is on the phone. Both look stoned, their bodies too relaxed for an ER.

I bang on the glass wall. "My arms and legs are tingling. My face is numb. I have that rare syndrome you can get from the flu shot."

"Calm down," the one with the long fingernails says.

"How can I calm down? I might be paralyzed in five minutes."

"Name?"

"Kimberlee Auerbach." Then I rattle off my birth date, address, my mother's name and number, before the woman has the chance to ask for any of it. The clicking of her nails on the keyboard makes me want to jump out of my skin, only I can't feel my skin.

"Okay. Have a seat," she says, waving me away without looking up.

I turn around and see an older couple with silver hair and walking canes and a little boy with his mommy. I sit down alone and scared, my life racing through my head the way it does in the movies. My mother. My father. My brother. My house in Tulsa, Oklahoma. Cindy Lauper. Le Clic cameras. Zach's beat-up burgundy car. Sharks and bats. The river in Costa Rica. The smell of Oaxacan chocolate. The #1 train. Seeing Noah ride up the escalator. The way I feel cuddling with him at night. How amazing he was during my brother's surgery. I think about the Death card and wonder if maybe Iris was wrong. What if it meant I was going to die? I can't feel my head. My arms are vibrating. My legs are tingling. It feels as if my finger is stuck in a live socket. What is happening to me? When are they going to call my name? What if by the time I see the doctor, it's too late? I think about my brother and all the times he had to go to the hospital as a little boy. Here I am thirty-three and freaking out. I can only imagine how scary it must have been for him. The pain. The fear. Afraid he might end up being paralyzed, and somewhere deep inside, thinking he might die. Of course he needed his mommy. This must be what Iris was talking about. Justice. Compassion. I get it. Now, please someone, call my goddamn name!

Noah rushes into the room and grabs my hand. "Are you okay?" he asks.

"I don't know," I say.

The nurse finally waves me over. Noah comes with me.

"What's your full name?" she asks.

"I already told that other woman," I say.

"Please tell me again," she asks with a fake smile.

What is wrong with you people?

"Kimberlee Dawn Auerbach," I say.

"Okay, Miss Auerbach. What are you feeling?"

"I already told the other woman—my arms and legs are tingling. My face is numb. I think I have that rare syndrome you can get from the flu shot."

"You got a flu shot?" she asks.

"Yes, earlier in the day."

She reaches over, takes my blood pressure, checks my temperature and then shuttles us to another waiting room, where we wait another hour.

"Why would they leave me unattended like this?" I ask Noah.

"I'm sure if they thought you were in real danger, they would have had a doctor look at you already. I'm sure you're fine."

The TV in the room is blaring, the man across from us is picking his ear, and Noah is flipping through an old *National Geographic* magazine when my brother walks into the room.

"Mikey!" I cry.

"Mom called and told me you were here," he says. "Are you okay?" He bends down to give me a hug and kiss, and then hugs Noah.

"Miss Auerbach?" a different nurse calls out.

"Here, we're here," my brother says.

She escorts us into a white room and tells us the doctor will be with us shortly.

Noah plants his hand on my shoulder. "How are you feeling, baby?"

"Same, I guess."

Mikey takes a plastic glove from the shelf and blows it up into a balloon. "This is what the nurses used to make for me when I was in the hospital," he says, handing me a white balloon hand.

"It kind of looks like the Hamburger Helper guy," I say, and laugh, my first laugh in over two hours.

The doctor walks into the room. He's tall and young, maybe even younger than me. "So tell me what's going on," he says, and sits down, crossing his legs.

"My arms and legs are tingling. My face is numb. I think I have that rare syndrome you can get from the flu shot," I say for the third time.

"Stand up," he says.

I stand.

"Touch your nose with your right pointer finger," he says.

I touch my nose with my right pointer finger.

"Touch your nose with your left pointer finger," he says.

I touch my nose with my left pointer finger.

"Now walk a straight line," he says.

"I feel wobbly," I say.

"It's okay. Take your time."

Mikey and Noah watch me take one step, then another step, then a third. The concern on their faces reminds me of a TV show I once saw about elephants. A baby elephant can't walk. Something is wrong with its legs. The other elephants keep trying to push the baby onto its feet. But nothing works. After three days, the pack of elephants must move on. You watch them start to walk away and then turn back, pushing the baby one more time. Finally, the baby stands and walks. They can all move on together.

"Well," the doctor says and gets up. "No motor function damage. No loss of eye-hand coordination. Miss Auerbach, I think—"

One of the nurses barges back in the room and says, "Numbness is the third most commonly reported side effect of this year's flu shot. Easily mistaken for Guillain-Barré syndrome."

Noah starts to cry and squeezes my arm. He had been strong for me the whole time, but he was worried too.

Mikey walks over and rubs my head. "You're going to be just fine, Kimmi." Then he reaches down to hug me good-bye. As I kiss his cheek, the one with the scar, I know we're going to be just fine too.

When Noah and I step outside, it's not yet midnight. It feels like a new day though. The air is crisp and clean. Everything looks brighter—the sparkling lights, people's faces, even the taxicabs. I still feel the tingling in my body, but it's almost orgasmic now. I am alive and breathing. Instead of feeling what I don't have, what I don't know, I feel peaceful, grateful. I feel everything. The wind on my cheeks. My hot breath. Noah's hand, my skin against his skin. I had been looking for comfort from an outside source, but *this moment* is my comfort.

As we walk to the garage to get the car, I feel like the Fool again, not knowing what will happen next, but this time I don't mind, I actually like it. This time I'm not going to hold on so tight.

Acknowledgments

I tried to write about the people in my life from a place of love and compassion and truth. I recognize that my recollection may differ from that of the other people who were in the room with me. My brother might swear it was this restaurant instead of that restaurant and he would probably be right. He has an amazing memory. And my mother might feel adamant that she didn't say that or in that tone or at least that's not what she meant. And my boyfriend may not remember saying that particular thing on that particular day in that particular way. And my father, well, he doesn't really care. Very little offends him. He has an uncanny ability not to take things personally. I wish I had inherited that trait. Anyway, I tried to stick closely to real dates, real places, indisputable events, but still, there will always be that one look, that one gesture, sentence, whatever, that is remembered differently, so in order to make the people I love the most in my life feel safer about being exposed in this book, I gave them veto rights. Anything they felt uncomfortable with, I either took out or changed. It takes a tremendous generosity of spirit and heart, especially for my boyfriend and family, to let me tell my story and subsequently their story in such a public way. For that, I will be forever grateful, indebted and awe-struck. There are some people I did not consult about being revealed in this book, so in order to protect their privacy, I changed some names, identifying features, details, etc. As for Iris Goldblatt, she is a composite, so I didn't have to check with her. She is based on a real tarot reader I used to see in the West Village and another tarot reader I once saw on the Upper West Side. And I've been collecting decks and reading tarot myself for over twelve years. So really, Iris is part downtown, part uptown, part me.

Thank you, Terry Lawler, Executive Director of New York Women in Film and Television, for connecting me with reporter Joe Hagan who wrote a snarky profile about me in the *New York Observer*. If it hadn't been for the article, Natalie Kaire, an editor at Warner Books, never would have called me. Thank you, Natalie, for being a friendly voice on a scary day. If Natalie hadn't liked my script she never would have connected me with my agent, Elisabeth Weed, who signed me on the spot. Thank you, Elisabeth, for believing in me with your whole heart and never giving up. You helped me change my life. Thank you to all the editors who came close to buying my book, but passed and to the two other editors who made offers. If my book hadn't gone to auction, I probably wouldn't have gotten enough money to quit my

acknowledgments

job. I will always be grateful to Dutton for rescuing me from the basement at Fox News Channel. I would especially like to thank Julie Doughty and Kara Cesare for both wanting my book. I feel blessed to have two great editors who double as margarita buddies. Thank you, Brian Tart, for giving the go-ahead and for being such a solid guy. And thank you, Julie, for deciding on hardcover and for helping me every step of the way. You were encouraging and comforting and always made me laugh. I couldn't dream of anyone better to help guide me through this process. Thank you, Amanda Tobier, Lisa Johnson, Beth Parker, the art department, the production team and everyone else at Dutton, for being behind this book and for helping me get the word out.

Thank you, Devan Sipher, for always making time for me, for reading carefully, for not accepting laziness and for pushing me beyond what I thought was possible. Thank you to my writers group (www.crucialminutia.com) for letting me present five times in a row. Your notes and comments and support really helped me get through the crunch. Courtney Martin, Kate Torgovnick, Jennifer Gandin Le, Ethan Todras-Whitehill, Felice Belle, Florian Duijsens, Joie Jager Hyman and Cristina Pippa—you have become family to me. Thank you, Mom, Eric Davis, Vivian Conan, Charles Salzberg, Marta Ravin, Lisa Hyman, Julia Neaman, Judy Davis and Molly May for reading my book and for giving me such great feedback. Thank you, Marta, for the great guacamole line. Thank you, Vivian, for the grammar lessons. Thank you, Tara Bracco, for making me understand when I was soliciting the reader for sympathy. I didn't know I was doing that until you showed me. Thank you, Diane Higgins, for your time and interest and for thinking I'm a good writer.

They say it takes a village to raise a child. Well, it took a village to write this book. Thank God this isn't an Oscar speech. I would be played off stage by now.

Now I have to thank my mentors. Thank you, Charles Salzberg, for teaching me how to write, for reading my material in all its various forms and for being so generous with me over the years. Thank you, Susan Shapiro, for taking me under your wing, for introducing me to Devan and for sharing your wisdom. You operate from such a place of abundance. It's beautiful. Thank you, Jay Fine, for being there in the beginning of my journey and for witnessing my growth.

Thank you, Wende Jager Hyman, Rashmi (Sasha) Sharma, Tiffany Shlain and the Woodhull Institute, for being so supportive of me and for helping women step into their power. You do good in the world. I feel proud to be a Woodhull alumni.

Thank you to everyone who gave me early blurbs: Naomi Wolf, Susan Shapiro, Sally Kaslow, Robin Stern, Stephanie Klein and Courtney Martin.

Thank you to everyone who helped me with my one-woman show, which is what inspired this book: Eric Davis, Scott C. Embler, Kirsten Ames, Kristen Caskey, Erin Keating, Charles Salzberg, Charlie Schulman, Christopher Roberts, Coleman Hough, Alicia Rancilio, The New York International Fringe Festival and Elena K. Holy.

acknowledgments

Thank you to my New York JCC writing workshop for helping me with my script: Charles Salzberg, Vivian Conan, Sally Kaslow, Ellen Schecter, Helen Zelon, Stephanie Klein, Marian Sabat, Betty Wald, Gloria Reina, Marilyn Goldstein, Sharon Gurwitz, Ricki Miller, Patricia Crevits, Sarah Doudna, Margaret Kennedy and Vicki Reggio.

Thank you to everyone at The Moth, especially to Catherine Burns, Lea Thau, Jennifer Hixon, Frank Damico and Andy Borowitz. The StorySLAM saved my life, gave me hope, built my self-esteem and offered me an opportunity to workshop my material.

I also need to thank Fox News Channel. I know I was unhappy there and often unpleasant. I know I played the victim and took it out on you. But the fact is that you were my family for almost nine years. You were good to me. You fed me, kept me warm and helped me grow up. I especially want to thank Fiona Martinelli, Karen Rush, Lisa Pincus, Ben Ramos, Matt Court, Marybeth Maher, Massoud Gamshad, Steve Ferri, Victor Verno, Brooke Lefferts, Alicia Rancilio, Sharon Fain, Maria Karlsson, Alisyn Camerota, Jennifer Murray, Tim Gaughan, Jonathan Wachtel, Anne Woolsey, Farhad Heydari, Megan O'Neill, Kevin Byrne, Janette Shaw, Kim Fargas, Don Collopy, Scott Wilder, Mike Fagan, Ron Messer, Randy Shimshak, Rob Galker, Jessica Rodriguez, Sharri Berg, Sherry Cheng, Jane Ziemski, Jon Brady, Carlos VanMeek, Shepard Smith, Billy Toth, Jason Scanlon, Dan Gallo, Mike Carpel, Mike Waco, Don Fair and Brian Jones.

Thank you, Marta Ravin and Max Leinwand, Jody

Speyer, Lisa and Joel Sackman, Marcus LeBov, Sarah Court, Matt Court and Marla Lehner, Amy and Bruce Humes, Lisa Pollard, Molly and Boris Skyar, Julia Neaman and David Klagsbrun, Stefanie Ziev, Wendy Shanker, Makeeba McCreary, Amy Jaffe and Jeff Brown, Evan Silverman, Karen Rush and Pete Rizzo, Fiona Martinelli, Lisa and Jordan Pincus, Ben Ramos, Sharon Fain, Angie Mills. Your friendships ground me and inspire me.

Thank you, Marta, for being the person I can call from a closet crying and for always, always making me laugh.

To my second family in the Valley: Judy, Allen, Lou, Jen, Asher and Izzy, thank you for all of your love and kindness.

Thank you, Guy Sliker and Samantha Wilt, Marpa Eager and Susan Pocharski, Oren Alkalay, Jesse Lenat, Dan and Marina Canale-Parola, Pablo Martin, Steve Ward, Arieh Kurinsky, Dmitri and Rebecca Robbins and Judy Ferber.

Thank you, John Gerson, for helping me love myself more. You healed something deep in me.

Thank you, Genpo Roshi, for giving the world Big Mind.

Thank you, Glenys Eldred, for showing me that the green field is inside me.

Thank you to everyone in my family: Michael and Michal; Lisa, Dan, Sophie and Jessie; David, Kelly, Josh, Ashley and Eliana; Ace, Barry, Adam and Andrew; Stacey and Kim; Shelly and Tony; Dad and Susan; Grandma and Grandpa; Auntie Kim and Uncle Jack; Nana; and Mom.

Mikey, I'm sorry I ever hurt you. I'm sorry I was so

jealous. I'm sorry for making home an unsafe place to be, especially when the world was often unkind to you. I love you and feel grateful to have you as my younger brother. Thank you for being so supportive and loving to me.

Dad, thank you for always being straight up with me. Your honesty and desire for me to be happy make me feel very loved. I love you and appreciate all of your help.

Mom, thank you for encouraging me to tell my story. Thank you for listening to me over the years, for loving me and for changing and growing and becoming the woman you've always wanted to be. I feel blessed, truly blessed and lucky, to have you as my mother. My love for you could fill the Universe.

An extra special thanks to my lover, partner, significant other, boyfriend, best friend, creative collaborator, "Noah." Thank you for being a man with integrity. I respect and admire that you didn't cave under pressure. You could have run for the hills when my father got an engagement ring, but you didn't. Thank you for staying in difficult times, for always being there for me, for loving me, for pushing me, for making me a better person and for helping me live my dream. This wouldn't have been possible without you. I love you and I always will.

About the Author

Kimberlee Auerbach is a writer and storyteller who has performed her comedic monologues throughout New York City at venues such as The Original Improv, The Kraine Theater and The Bitter End. Her one-woman show played to sold-out houses at the New York International Fringe Festival and she has competed in several Moth GrandSLAM Championships. She lives in New York City.